WordPress for Beginners

A Visual Step-by-Step Guide to Creating your
Own WordPress Site in Record Time, Starting from Zero!

Dr. Andy Williams

http://ezseonews.com

Covering Wordpress 4

Updated 27st October 2014

What people are saying about this book:

"I work in the education department at one of the top academic institutions in the U.S. and if I could hire Dr. Williams to write all of my online training, I wouldn't hesitate." **Laura**

"Another fine book from Dr. Andy. " **Mr. Bearly**

"Wow! I am not new to WordPress but I love this book." **Albert J**

"Fantastic WordPress Guide! I highly recommend this guide to anyone - new or experienced - because he points out the little things that make a WordPress site fun and rewarding!" **Dawn Carter**

"This screenshot-based book makes it drop-dead simple to create a site. Screenshots allow you to make sure your screen looks like the one in the book." **James E. Hunter**

"I've only gotten partway through this book and had to stop to say how impressed I am! If I had this a few weeks ago I'm sure I would have had my site up & running by now. I love how Mr. Williams uses screen shots and guides you through the process step by step. His explanations are easy to understand & his instructions are easy to follow. I can't believe how much more I understand about WordPress & setting up a site now than I did just a few hours ago. I would highly recommend this book to anyone whose using WordPress for the first time (or even the second, third or fourth time!!). It will save you hours of time and frustration and make the whole process so much easier." **gail87821**

"Another Masterpiece from Doc Andy!" **David Harvey**

"..Then I found WordPress for Beginners and WOW - my progress took off. Having a visual guide with extensive photos really helps those of us who are visual learners. But the best thing to me is that Williams not only describes what to do and how to do it, he explains why you should do it. I'm not a professional tech person

and this book is exactly what I needed. I suspect I will continue to refer to it in the future. Highly recommended." *SamanthaSSJ*

"If you want to have a website but don't know how, this book by Dr. Andy Williams will take you by the hand and walk you through the process of setting up your own blog correctly. He tells you not only exactly how to do it, but also explains the why you are taking the steps he walks you through. The instructions and visuals are clear and easy for anyone to follow." *J. Tanner*

"Dr. Andy Williams released another winner friends! Knowing Andy is a trusted teacher and internet expert I jumped on the opportunity to learn, study and apply WordPress for Beginners. It amazes me how much hype, bogus information and garbage there is on the market today about WordPress - but where do you go to get the real deal? This is exactly what you get with Andy's work - the real deal." *Chris Cobb*

DISCLAIMER AND TERMS OF USE AGREEMENT

Contents

Who am I & why should you listen to me?

My name is Andy Williams and I am a teacher. In 2001 I gave up teaching in schools where I had been a Science teacher working with students from 11 to 18 years of age. I needed a new challenge, and most of all I wanted to spend more time with my family.

Since then my work (and my hobby), has been to study the search engines and build websites for profit. It's been a long journey and a large number of people have followed me on that passage by reading my free weekly newsletter published over at ezSEONews.com. My newsletter has covered a wide range of topics relevant to webmasters - that's people who own and build their own website(s). If you are interested, you can sign up to receive my free newsletter too.

In the early days, websites were hand-built using a code called Hyper Text Markup Language, or HTML for short. To create good-looking websites you needed to be something of a geek. Tools like Macromedia Dreamweaver (now owned by Adobe), and Microsoft Front Page (discontinued in 2006), were developed to reduce the coding learning curve associated with building a website in HTML, but these tools were expensive.

Then in May 2003, Matt Mullenweg & Mike Little, released a tool that would change the face of website building forever. They called it WordPress.

I have to admit to being a little reluctant to give up my copy of Dreamweaver, but in 2004 I started to experiment with the WordPress platform. At that time, WordPress was just starting to get interesting with the introduction of "plugins". Don't worry, we'll look at those later in the book, but for now just understand that plugins are an easy and pain-free ways of adding great new functionality to your website.

Fast-forward to today and WordPress is now the site-building tool of choice for many professionals and enthusiasts alike. For example; home businesses run by moms & dads, school kids running blogs about their favorite bands, large corporations, and everyone in between, have all turned to WordPress. It's extremely powerful, flexible, produces very professional looking websites or blogs, is relatively easy to use, and perhaps best of all, it's totally free.

Sure, there is a learning curve, but that is where I come in.

With years of experience teaching technical stuff in an easy to understand manner, I am going to take you by the hand and guide you as you construct your very own professional looking website or blog, even if you know absolutely nothing about how to go about this. The only thing you need to know is how to use a web browser. So if you have ever searched Google for something, then you already have the skills necessary to follow this book.

I have made this book a step-by-step, visual guide to creating your website. Just follow along with the exercises, and in no time at all you'll be using WordPress like a pro as you build a website you can be proud to show your family and friends. In fact, they will probably start asking YOU to help them build their own projects.

Excited?

OK, let's get on with it.

How to Use this Book

I have written this book as a hands-on tutorial. To get the most out of it, I recommend that you sit at your computer, following the steps outlined in its pages. Whenever I do something on my demo site, you then do it on your own site. Don't be afraid of making mistakes; just have fun and experiment with WordPress. Mistakes can easily be undone or deleted, and anyway, most of us learn better by making a few blunders along the way.

By the end of this book you will have a solid understanding of how WordPress works and how you can get it to do what YOU want it to do. If you then decide to take your WordPress knowledge to the next level, you'll have an excellent foundation from which to build upon.

What is WordPress?

WordPress is a Content Management System (CMS). That just means it is a piece of software that can help you manage and organize your content into an impressive and coherent website.

Initially WordPress was created as a blogging tool, but over the years it has become so much more than that. Today, many WordPress driven sites look nothing like blogs (unless that's what the user wants). This is down to the flexibility of this amazing tool.

WordPress powers simple blogs, corporate websites and everything in between. Companies like Sony, the Wall Street Journal, Samsung, New York Times, Wired, CNN, Forbes, Reuters and many others, all use WordPress as part of their online presence.

WordPress is 'open source', meaning that all of its code is free to use and customize. This is one of the powers of WordPress, since programmers the world over have created their own additions to this powerful publishing platform; from website templates to plugins that extend the functionality of this amazing site building tool.

Some of the features that make WordPress great

• Template system for site design means that changing the look and feel of your site is as simple as installing a new theme. There's a plethora of free and quality WordPress themes available.

• Plugins are pieces of code that you can download into your WordPress site to add new features and functions. There are literally thousands of plugins available and many are totally free.

• Once it is set up, you can concentrate on adding great content to your site. You simply type it into a text editor within the WordPress Dashboard, hit publish, and WordPress takes care of the rest.

• WordPress also has a feature called Widgets that allows the user to drag and drop "features" and place them in, for example, the sidebar. You may have a widget that allows you to display a poll to your visitors – for example. You can place that poll in the sidebar of your site by dragging the poll widget to the appropriate place. Widgets are typically used in the sidebars, but some templates allow widgets to be placed in the site footer as well as on the homepage. We will look at widgets in much more detail later on in this book.

• WordPress can help you with the SEO (Search Engine Optimization), of your site, so that it has the potential to rank better in search engines like Google and BING.

WordPress.com v WordPress.org

There are actually two "flavours" of WordPress. Firstly there is WordPress from WordPress.com. The second one is WordPress from WordPress.org.

It is vital that you understand the difference between these two.

WordPress.com

WordPress.com allows anyone to sign up for a free WordPress site that WordPress will host on *their* servers. All you need to provide is the content for the site.

Example: Say you wanted to create a website on "educational toys for kids". You could set up a website called educationaltoysforkids.wordpress.com (assuming no one else has taken that address (name), already).

Your website address (URL) would be:

educationaltoysforkids.wordpress.com

.. and by visiting that address in your web browser, you'd see the homepage of your site.

What you actually have is a sub-domain on the wordpress.com domain.

The problem with this is that you do not own the site, Wordpress.com do. One day you might go to look at your site and find that it's no longer there.

There is also a number of restrictions onWordPress.com. For example, there are some plugins you won't be able to install and you'll also have a limited choice of themes/templates.

For these reasons, I do not recommend you create your site on WordPress.com. This book will assume you are going to use the other WordPress – the one from WordPress.org.

WordPress.org

WordPress.org is a site where you can download your own copy of WordPress for free. You can then upload that copy of WordPress to any web server you like and start building a site that YOU own. You will also be able to choose whatever domain name you like, so you could call your site educationaltoysforkids.com (if it's available). Doesn't that look more professional than the options on WordPress.com?

Think of the difference between WordPress.com and WordPress.org as being similar to renting or owning a house. When you rent a house, there are limits to what you can do to it. You can be thrown out at any time. When you own the building outright, you can do whatever you want with it and no one can tell you how to design, decorate, or renovate *your* home.

The only disadvantages of using WordPress from WordPress.com are the costs involved. These costs are minimal though, so let's look at them now.

The costs of owning your own site

So how much is a website going to cost you? As you build your site there will be optional costs - things like a website theme, autoresponder or mailing list, but these are totally optional since most things can be done for free. However, there are two costs that you cannot avoid.

The website domain

The website domain is your site's address on the internet. **Google.com** is the website domain of our favourite search engine. **CNN.com** is the domain of a popular international news service.

You will need to buy a domain for your website. We'll look at this later, but for now, let's just consider the price. Typically a domain name will cost around $10 per year. You can sometimes get the first year for free when you buy web hosting, but once that first year is up, you'll be paying the $10 per year to keep your domain name live.

Your domain name will be registered with a company called a registrar. It is this registrar that will collect the $10 payment every year. The registrar can actually be the same company that you use for your web hosting, or a different company. We'll look at the pros and cons of both options.

Website hosting

Your website needs to be on a computer somewhere that is attached to the internet 24/7 so that people can find it. We call these computers "web servers" and companies that lease, rent or buy them are called web hosts. Their job is to make sure the servers are up, running, and well maintained at all times. You therefore need to rent some disk space on one of these servers to hold your website. We rent server space from a web hosting company. This is a monthly fee of around $5 per month (although it does vary greatly between web hosts).

As mentioned earlier, some web hosts offer a free domain name (for the first year). They can offer a free domain name because you are paying them a monthly fee for the web hosting; therefore they get their investment back over time. In order to take advantage of the free domain offers, you will need to use your web host as the registrar for your domain.

The total essential costs of running your own website are therefore around $70 per year.

Registrar & web hosts

When you sign up with a web host, you have the choice to let them be the registrar for your website as well. The advantage of this is that all payments you need to make are to the same company, meaning you only have to deal with ONE outfit.

There are disadvantages to this arrangement though, and a lot of people (including myself), prefer to keep host and registrar separate.

Potential problem: If for any reason your web host decides your website is causing them problems (i.e. they get spam complaints, or your website is using up too many system resources), they can take your site down without any warning. What happens next?

Let's look at what happens if you use your web host as registrar.

1. Your site goes down.
2. You contact your host and they tell you that they received spam complaints from your domain.
3. They refuse to put your site back up.
4. You need to move your site to a new host, but your existing host is the registrar and can make that difficult.
5. Your site remains down for a long period of time while you sort things out, and eventually move the site to a new host and registrar.

OK, let's look at what happens if your registrar is separate from your host.

1. Your site goes down.
2. You contact your host and they tell you that they received spam complaints from your domain.
3. They refuse to put your site back up.
4. You order hosting at a new host, and copy your site to the new host.
5. You login to your registrar account and change the name servers (don't worry about this, we'll look at it later), to the new host. This takes seconds to do.
6. Your site is back up within 24 hours or sooner.

This is one scenario where using a separate host and registrar is important.

Another scenario, which doesn't bear thinking about, is if your hosting company goes out of business (it does happen sometimes). So what becomes of your site? Well, you probably lose it AND your domain name if your hosting company is also your registrar.

If your registrar and host are with two separate companies, and this happened, you'd simply get hosting somewhere else and change the name servers at your registrar. With this arrangement, your site would only be down for 24 hours or less.

Another situation that I have heard about is when a hosting company locks you out of your control panel (a login area where you can administer your domain(s)), because of a dispute over something. That means you cannot possibly move the domain to a new host, because you must have access to that control panel to do it. Consequently your domain will be down for as long as the dispute takes to resolve.

A final word of caution! I have heard horror stories of people not being able to transfer their domain out from a bad webhost. Even worse than that, the domain they registered at the hosting company was not registered in their name, but in the name of the hosting company. I therefore recommend that when you are ready to buy hosting, you consider the web host and registrar that I personally use.

I also recommend that you use a separate registrar and ignore those "free for the first year" offers. However, if you just want the easy option of using one company, use the web host I recommend. I have used them for years (sometimes as a combined host and registrar on a few sites), and never had a problem.

Recommended registrars & webhosts

Since the details (prices, features, etc.), of web hosts in particular, can change so much, I have created a page on my website that list the currently recommended web hosts and registrars.

On that page you'll find out about the features and prices.

Check out my recommended web host and domain registrar:

http://ezseonews.com/dwh

While you are there, you might like to sign up for my free weekly newsletter.

Tasks to complete

1. Sign up for web hosting. If you are going to use a separate registrar, sign up for the registrar first and buy the domain name. Once that is cleared, go and sign up for web hosting and point the domain at your new web server by changing the DNS. Instructions to do this are given on the webpage I mentioned above.

Installing WordPress

For this, you need to login to the cPanel of your hosting. The URL, username and password were all in the welcome email the host sent you when you signed up.

Once you are logged in, scroll down to the **Software/Services** section, and click on **Softaculous.**

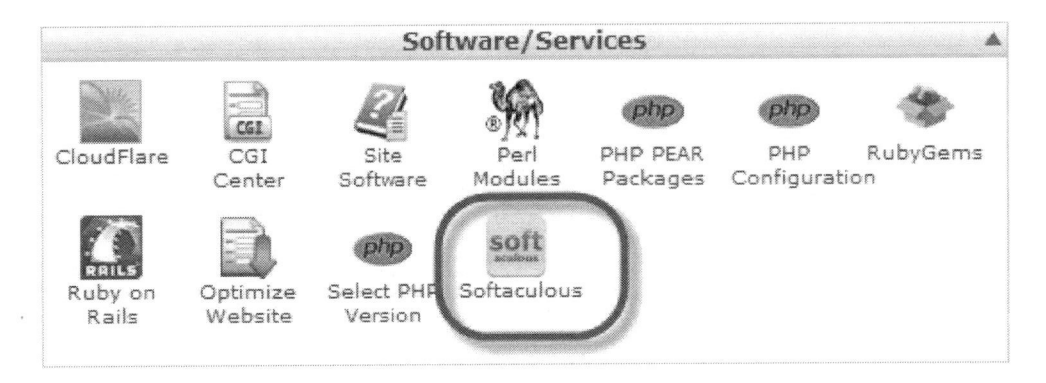

On the next screen, you'll see a box containing the Wordpress logo. Move your mouse over it, and an **Install** button will appear:

WordPress
★★★★★

WordPress is a state-of-the-art publishing platform with a focus on aesthetics, web standards, and usability.

Install   Demo

Click the **Install** button.

At the top of the next screen, you'll see this:

Software Setup

Choose Protocol
If your site has SSL, then please choose the HTTPS protocol.

http:// ▼

Choose Domain
Please choose the domain to install the software.

rapidwpsites.com

In Directory
The directory is relative to your domain and **should not exist**.
e.g. To install at http://mydomain/dir/ just type **dir**. To install only
in http://mydomain/ leave this empty.

Database Name
Type the name of the database to be created for the installation

wpRWPS

In the **"Choose Domain"** box, select your domain.

In the **"In Directory"** box, delete the pre-filled value, leaving this empty.

Under **"Database Name"**, you can leave this as the default value. I personally change it a little, so I know which database in my account belongs to which website, but that is because I have a number of sites in my hosting package.

Next we have these settings:

Database Settings

Table Prefix

wp_

Site Settings

Site Name

Rapid WP Sites

Site Description

urces and help with Wordpress

Enable Multisite (WPMU)
This feature will Enable Multisite option for your WordPress blog.
Your server must support Apache mod_rewrite to use this feature.

You can leave the table prefix as it is. I always change mine, just to make it more difficult for hackers that might be trying to hack my site. wp_ is the default value, and hackers know this. If you want, change it to a different 2 or 3 letters, followed by an underscore.

Enter a name & description for your site. You can change these later, so don't worry too much about it.

Leave Enable Multisite (WPMU) unchecked.

Next we have the Admin account settings:

Admin Account

Admin Username	admin
Admin Password	pass
	Bad (18/100)
Admin Email	admin@rapidwpsites.com

Don't use admin as your username. Again, this is the default and makes it easier for hackers. Change your admin username to something else. Also add a strong password. This username and password combination will be used to login to your Wordpress Dashboard, so make a note of what you enter here. The "Admin email" box will set the admin email in your Wordpress dashboard, and this will be used to notify you of events, like people leaving comments. This can be changed later.

By default, the language will be set to English, but change this if you need to.

Select Plugins

Limit Login Attempts
If selected Limit Login Attempts plugin will be installed and activated with your installation.
Click here to visit plugin site.

☑

➕ **Advanced Options**

Disable Update Notifications
If checked you will not receive an email notification for updates available for this installation.

☐

Auto Upgrade
If checked, this installation will be automatically upgraded to the latest version when a new version is available.

☐

Automated backups
Softaculous will take automated backups via CRON as per the frequency you select

Once a month ▼

Backup Rotation
If the backup rotation limit is reached Softaculous will delete the oldest backup for this installation and create a new backup. The backups will utilize your space so choose the backup rotation as per the space available on your server

4 ▼

Install

Email installation details to :

Check the box next to **"Limit Login Attempts"**. This is another layer of protection against hackers.

Under the **"Advanced Options"**, select **"Once a Month"** for automated backups (or more frequently if you will be adding content on a daily basis).

The "Backup Rotation" is the number of backups the host will keep for you. Once that number of backups has been created, the oldest will be deleted to make room for the new backup. On a monthly backup schedule, 4 is about right. If you are backing up more frequently, choose a larger number of backups.

Finally, enter your email address at the bottom before clicking the install button. You Wordpress login details will be emailed to you at this address when Wordpress is installed.

OK, once the installation has finished, you'll be shown something like this:

Congratulations, the software was installed successfully

WordPress has been successfully installed at :
http://rapidwpsites.com
Administrative URL : http://rapidwpsites.com/wp-admin/

We hope the installation process was easy.

NOTE: Softaculous is just an automatic software installer and does not prov
visit the software vendor's web site for support!

Regards,

The first link will load your website (currently a skeleton site created by Wordpress). Here is mine:

Yours will probably look very similar.

The second URL listed is the Administrative URL. You can click that link to login to the Wordpress Dashboard for your site. The username and password are those that you used when filling in the Admin Details a few minutes ago.

Go check out your site

Go and look at your website in a web browser by typing in the domain URL into the address bar.

You should see your WordPress site up and running. Of course, it won't have any of your content yet and it does come pre-installed with a few pages you'll need to delete, but you should see the homepage displaying a "Hello World!" post.

Before we start learning how to configure the site, let's just login, and then logout again, so we know how.

You should have made a note of the login URL, but if not, just add **/wp-login.php** to the end of your domain name (you can also access the site by adding **/wp-admin** to the end of the URL), e.g.

http://mydomain.com/wp-login.php

or

http://mydomain.com/wp-admin

You'll be taken to the login screen:

WORDPRESS

Username

andy ⬅

Password

•••••••••••••••••••• ⬅

☑ Remember Me   Log In

Lost your password?

← Back to Visual Wordpress

Enter the username and password you chose when you were installing WordPress then click the "Log In" button.

I also recommend you check the "Remember Me" box so that your username and password will be automatically entered next time you come to login to your Dashboard.

NOTE: If you ever forget your password, you can click the link under the login boxes to get the password resent to your admin email address (that's the one you entered when installing WordPress).

After logging in, you will now find yourself inside your Dashboard. You can have a look around but don't go changing anything just yet. Don't worry if it looks a little daunting in there. We'll take a tour of the Dashboard and I'll show you step-by-step, with screenshots, how to set it all up so you can have a great looking website.

NOTE: You will more than likely have notifications that there are some plugins (and even WordPress itself), that need updating. We'll do that in a moment. For now, let's log out so you are clear on how to do that.

Move your mouse over the top right where it says "Howdy Yourname". A menu will appear:

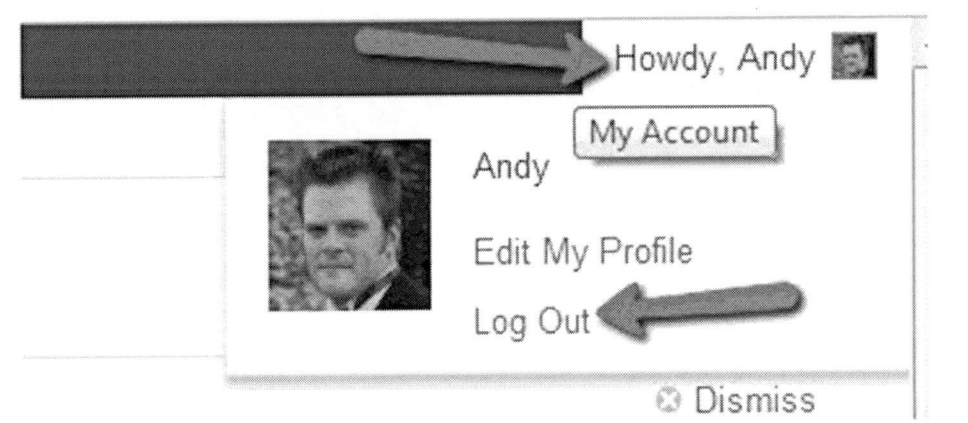

Click the "Log Out" link and you'll be logged out and taken back to the login screen.

Great, WordPress is installed and you now know how to login and logout of your Dashboard.

In the next section we'll take a tour of the Dashboard so you can get your bearings.

Tasks to complete

1. Install WordPress.
2. Login, have a quick look around the Dashboard, then logout again.

Installing the Twenty Eleven Theme

Every year or so, Wordpress releases a new default theme. Currently that theme is Twenty Fourteen. However, to get you up and running, I am going to stick to Twenty Eleven in this book. Although it is a few years old, it is easy to handle and ideal for Wordpress beginners. Once you have gone through this book, working with Twenty Eleven, you can switch your site over to the latest default Wordpress template (or any other template you want to use), and start having fun making your site look the way YOU want it to look.

Chances are, you won't have Twenty Eleven installed in your Wordpress Dashboard, so that is the first thing we are going to do.

Before you do though, go and look at your site homepage. Once we have installed and activated the Twenty Eleven theme, the appearance will change. You are about to see how easy it is to change the look and feel of your site, just by installing a new theme.

First thing to do is click on the **Themes** menu inside the **Appearance** menu:

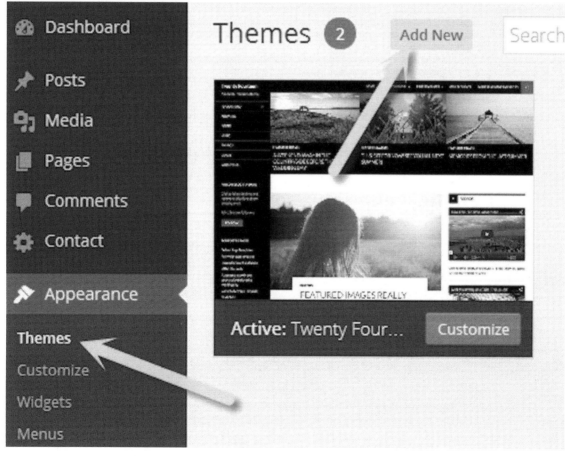

You will see an **Add New** button at the top. Click it.

You can now enter the theme name into the search box, and click the Search button. Search for **Twenty Eleven.**

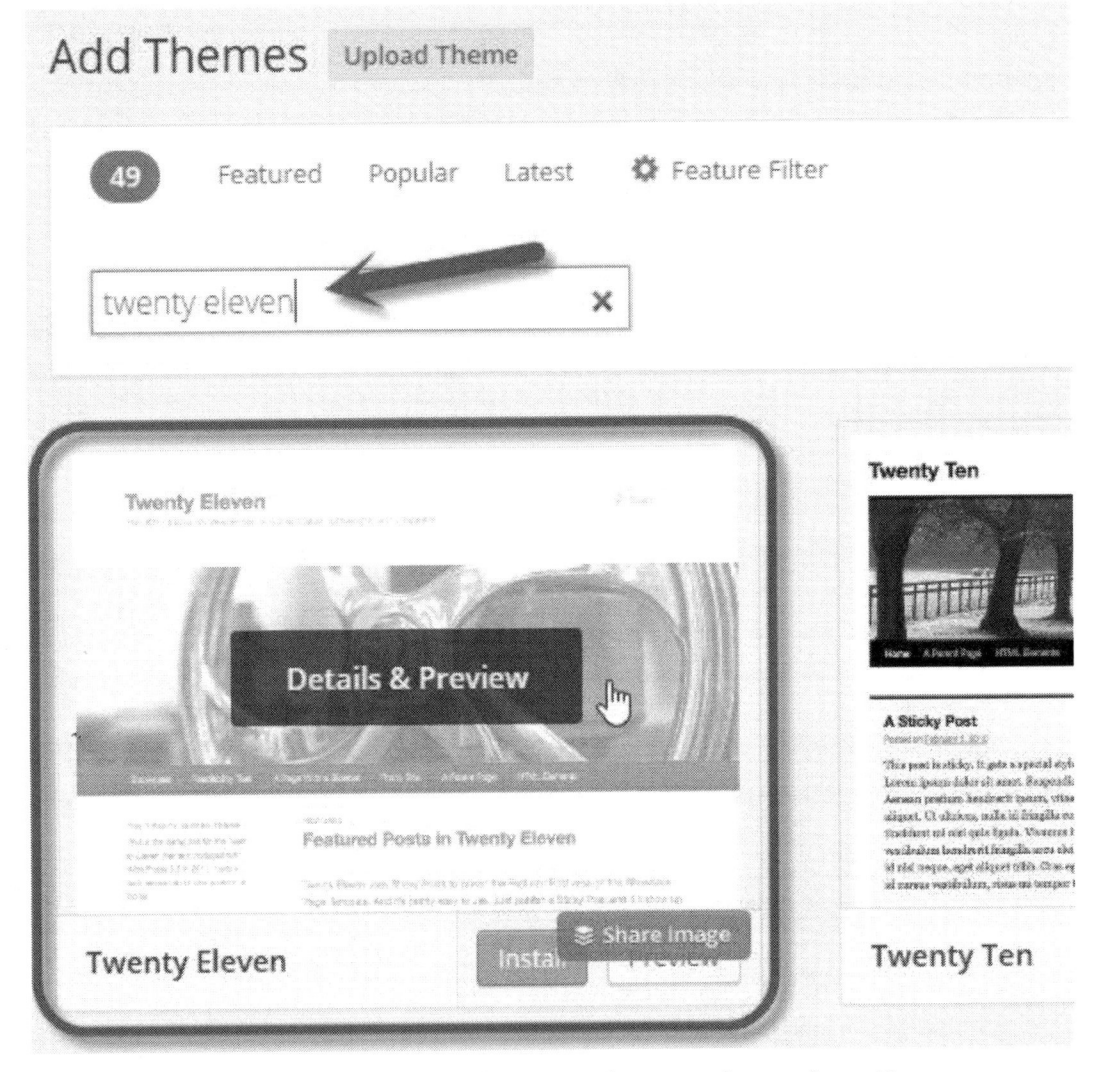

You will see the Twenty Eleven theme in the search results. Move your mouse over the thumbnail of the theme, and you'll see options to Install or Preview the theme. There will also be a large "Details & Preview" button in the middle that you can click if you want more information about a theme.

Click the **Install** button.

The theme will install. Once done, there will be a link to **Activate** the theme. Click the activate link.

If you now visit your site homepage, you will see the Twenty Eleven theme installed on your site.

That is how easy it is to change the look and feel of your site. OK, now the theme is installed, let's get on.

An overview of the Dashboard

When you login to WordPress, you are presented with the Dashboard. This is what it looks like:

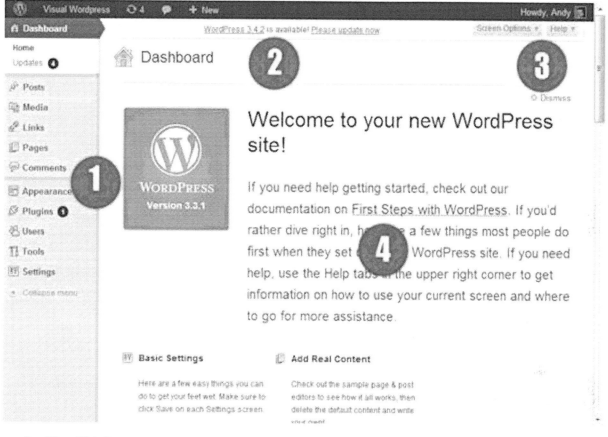

1. The Sidebar
2. Update Notification
3. Screen Options, Help, Profile & Logout
4. The Main screen

Let's look at each of these in turn.

The sidebar

The sidebar is the main navigation system of your Dashboard. From the sidebar, you can set up your website to look and behave as you want it to. This is where you can add/edit content on your site, upload images, moderate comments, change your site theme, add/remove plugins, and everything else you will need to do as a website owner. We'll look at all of these features in detail later in the tutorial.

Update notification

Occasionally you'll see a notification in this area to tell you that there is an update to WordPress. Whenever you see an update notification, it is a good idea to update your installation (we'll see how to do that later). This will ensure your site has the latest bug fixes and enhancements that the new version of WordPress brings. Be aware that hackers can take advantage of vulnerabilities in the WordPress security, and as WordPress finds out about these vulnerabilities, they fix them and release an update. Therefore, always update whenever you see the notification.

Screen options, help, profile & logout

Screen Options is a drop down menu that allows you decide what is shown on the various screens within the Dashboard. If you click the Screen Options link you'll see something like this:

Show on screen

☑ Right Now ☑ Pretty Link Quick Add ☑ Recent Comments ☑ Incoming Links ☑ Plugins ☑ QuickPress

☑ Recent Drafts ☑ WordPress Blog ☑ Other WordPress News ☐ Welcome

Screen Layout

Number of Columns: ○ 1 ◉ 2

What you see will depend on where you are in the dashboard (and what version of Wordpress you are using), because the options that are shown are relevant to the current page you are viewing. For example, if you are in section for moderating comments, the screen options you will see will be relevant to commenting.

By checking the boxes in the screen options, you display those sections on the page. If you don't want to see something you simply uncheck it. For example, to hide "WordPress News",

Save Draft

WordPress News

WordPress 3.8 "Parker"   December 12, 2013

Version 3.8 of WordPress, named "Parker" in honor of Charlie Parker, bebop innovator, is available for download or update in your WordPress dashboard. We hope you'll think this is the most beautiful update yet. Introducing a modern new design WordPress has gotten a facelift. 3.8 brings a fresh new look to the entire admin dashboard. […]

WPTavern: Opus: A Free WordPress Blogging Theme With A Big Personality

Joseph: WordPress Car Stickers

WPTavern: WordPress Developers Take Note: TinyMCE 4.0 Merged Into Core

Popular Plugin: Captcha (Install)

Version 3.8

just uncheck it in the Screen Options, and that section of the page will disappear.

Show on screen

✔ At a Glance   ✔ Activity   ✔ Quick Draft   ☐ WordPress News   ✔ Welcome

Dashboard

If you find that something is missing from the screen in a certain part of the dashboard, go in and check the screen options to ensure that it's enabled. We will be popping into the screen options a few times during this book.

To the right of the Screen options button is a button to access WordPress help. Clicking it opens up a help panel:

Overview	Welcome to your WordPress Dashboard!	**For more information:**
Navigation	This is the screen you will see when you log in to your site, and gives you access to all	Documentation on Dashboard
Layout	the site management features of WordPress. You can get help for any screen	Support Forums
Content	by clicking the Help tab in the upper corner.	

Help ▲

🏠 Dashboard

The left side of this help panel is tabbed, offering you help sections on various aspects of the Dashboard like navigation & layout. If you need more detailed help, there are links on the right side which point to the WordPress support forums and more

Dashboard documentation.

Finally in this area of the Dashboard screen, if you place your mouse over the "Howdy Yourname" top right, a panel opens up:

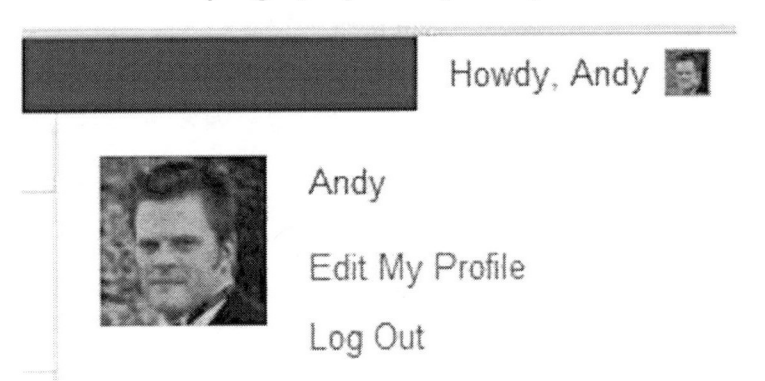

NOTE: Mine shows a photo of myself. I'll show you how & why later when we look at Gravatars in the User Profile section of the book.

This section of the Dashboard gives you a direct link to your profile (which we will fill out later), and a link to logout of your WordPress Dashboard. Whenever you finish a session in the WordPress Dashboard, it's always a good idea to log out.

The main screen

This is where all of the work takes place. What you see in the main screen area will depend on where you are in the Dashboard. For example, if you are in the comments section, the main screen area will list all the comments people have made on your site. If you are in the appearance section of your Dashboard, the main screen section will show you the theme/template of your site. If you are adding or editing a post, the main screen area will have everything you need to add/edit a post.

Tasks to complete

1. Go in and explore the Dashboard to familiarize yourself with the system.
2. Click on a few of the menu items in the left navigation column and then open the screen options to see what it contains. See how the options are related to the page you are viewing in the Dashboard?
3. Have a look at the help options - the forum and the other WordPress documentation. You won't need any of that now, but it is a good idea to be familiar with these options just in case you get stuck in the future.

Cleaning out the preinstalled stuff

When you install WordPress, it installs a few default items like the "Hello World" post you saw on the homepage earlier. In addition to that post, there is a "Sample page", a comment, and some widgets.

NOTE: WordPress allows you to create two types of content - posts and pages. Don't worry about the differences between these just yet as we'll look at them later.

OK, let's clean out the preinstalled stuff.

Deleting the "Hello World" post

This is the first thing we need to delete. If you visit your site homepage right now - before deleting it - you'll see that the "Hello World" post is displayed front and centre.

To delete the post, we need to open the "Posts" menu from the left hand sidebar navigation:

To do this you can either click the word "posts", or just hover your mouse over it. With the menu open, click the "All Posts" link.

This will open up a table of all posts on your site:

	Title	Author	Categories	Tags	💬	Date
☐	Hello world! Edit | Quick Edit | Trash | View	Andy	Uncategorized	No Tags	💬	2012/10/15 Publishe d
☐	Title	Author	Categories	Tags	💬	Date

Under "Title" you'll see the "Hello World!" post. Move your mouse over the title and a menu appears underneath the title.

This menu allows you to:

1. Edit the post

2. Quick Edit - which allows you to edit title, category, etc., but not the content of the post.
3. Move the post to Trash (i.e. delete it).
4. View the post – which will open the post in the current browser window.

We want to delete the post, so click on the "Trash" link. The screen will refresh and the post will be gone.

NOTE: I am going to keep the "Hello World!" post on my site so that I can use it later in the book. If you want to keep it for now as well, you can. When you need to delete it, you know how.

If you delete a post by accident, don't worry. At the top of the screen, you'll see a link to the Trash.

In the screenshot above, you'll see that there is a (1) next to the Trash link. That means there is one item in the trash. If you click on the Trash link, you'll be taken to the trash bin where you can see all of the posts that were sent to there.

All (0) | **Trash** (1)

Bulk Actions ▾   Apply

Show all dates ▾   View all categories ▾

☐	Title	Author
☐	**Hello world!**	Andy
	Restore	Delete Permanently	
☐	Title	Author

Bulk Actions ▾   Apply   Empty Trash

If you mouse-over the post title, you'll get another popup menu. This one allows you to restore the post (i.e. undelete it), or delete it permanently.

If you have a lot of posts in the trash and you want to delete them all, click the "Empty Trash" button at the bottom.

When WordPress created the "Hello World!" post, it also added a comment to it. When you deleted the post, the comment was also deleted because it belonged to that post.

OK, that's the Hello World post gone. Let's now get onto that sample page.

Deleting the sample page

In the sidebar navigation of your Dashboard, click on the Pages link. Again, you can click directly on the link, or mouse-over to open the menu. Click on "All Pages".

Like the posts section, this will bring up a list of all pages on the site. Mouse over the Sample page title, and click the Trash link underneath it.

Deleting widgets

WordPress pre-configured your website with a number of widgets in the sidebar of your website. You can see them if you look at your website:

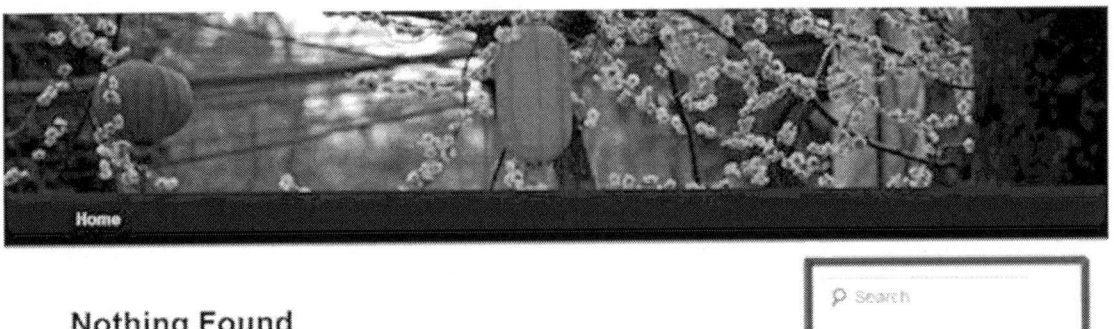

Those are widgets on the right. Let's delete them.

In your Dashboard, move your mouse over the Appearance menu, and click on Widgets:

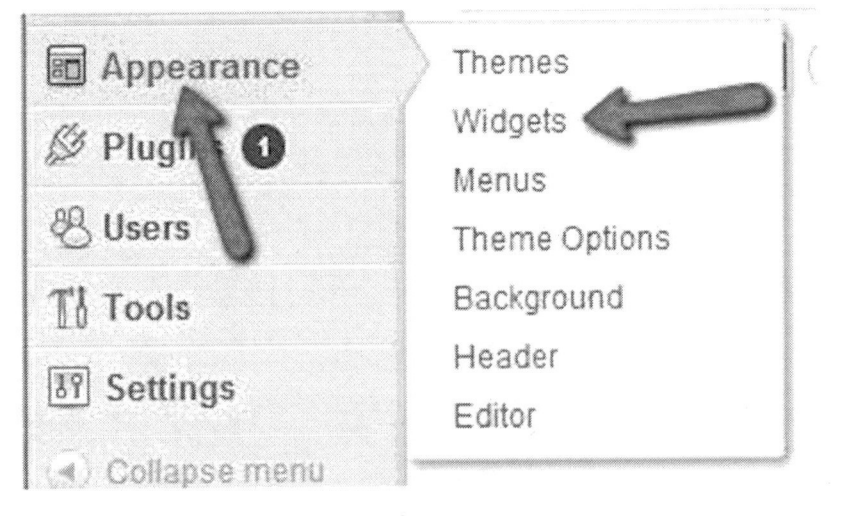

This will take you to the widget screen:

The screen is split into two sections. On the left you'll see the "available widgets". You can insert these into the sidebar of your site by dragging and dropping them onto a widgetized area listed on the right. Be aware that different templates have different widgetized areas, so if you are not using the Twenty Eleven theme from Wordpress, you will be seeing something a little different on the right hand side.

So what is a widgetized area?

It's simply an area of your webpage that allows you to insert something (in the form of a widget). E.g. your site sidebar is a widgetized area that allows you to add any widgets you like. When you installed WordPress, there were several widgets added here by default.

You will also notice on the right that there are widgetized areas called "Footer Area One", "Footer Area Two" and "Footer Area Three". This means you can add widgets to the footer (left, middle and right side of the footer), with this particular WordPress template/theme.

NOTE: All WordPress templates/themes are different. Not all templates will allow you to place widgets in the footer and some templates will allow widgets in areas that this default template doesn't. The best way to find out where each widgetized area is on the website is to consult the documentation that came with your theme or just add a widget and see where it appears.

WordPress installed several widgets into the "Main Sidebar" area of your site.

The widgets you see above are: Search, recent posts, recent comments, archives, categories and Meta.

Each installed Widget has a small downward-pointing arrow next to it on the right. Click this arrow to open up the settings for that particular widget:

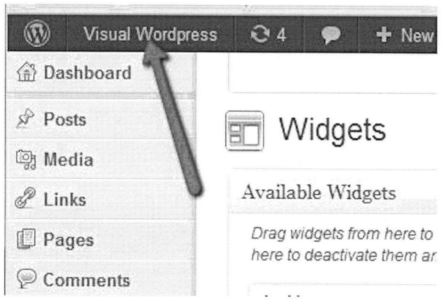

You'll see that there are a couple of options available for this "Recent Comments" widget. You can enter a title (leaving this blank will use the default title for the widget, in this case "Recent Comments"). You can also specify how many comments to show. This one is set to 5.

To delete the widget, click the Delete link bottom left.

The widget will disappear from the Main Sidebar area. Repeat to delete all of the other widgets. The only one I am leaving in my install for now is the Meta widget. This gives me an easy link to login to my site from the homepage, so I'll keep it there for now. You can do the same if you wish.

OK, we are done cleaning out WordPress.

Click the link to your homepage (top left of the dashboard) to see what your site now looks like:

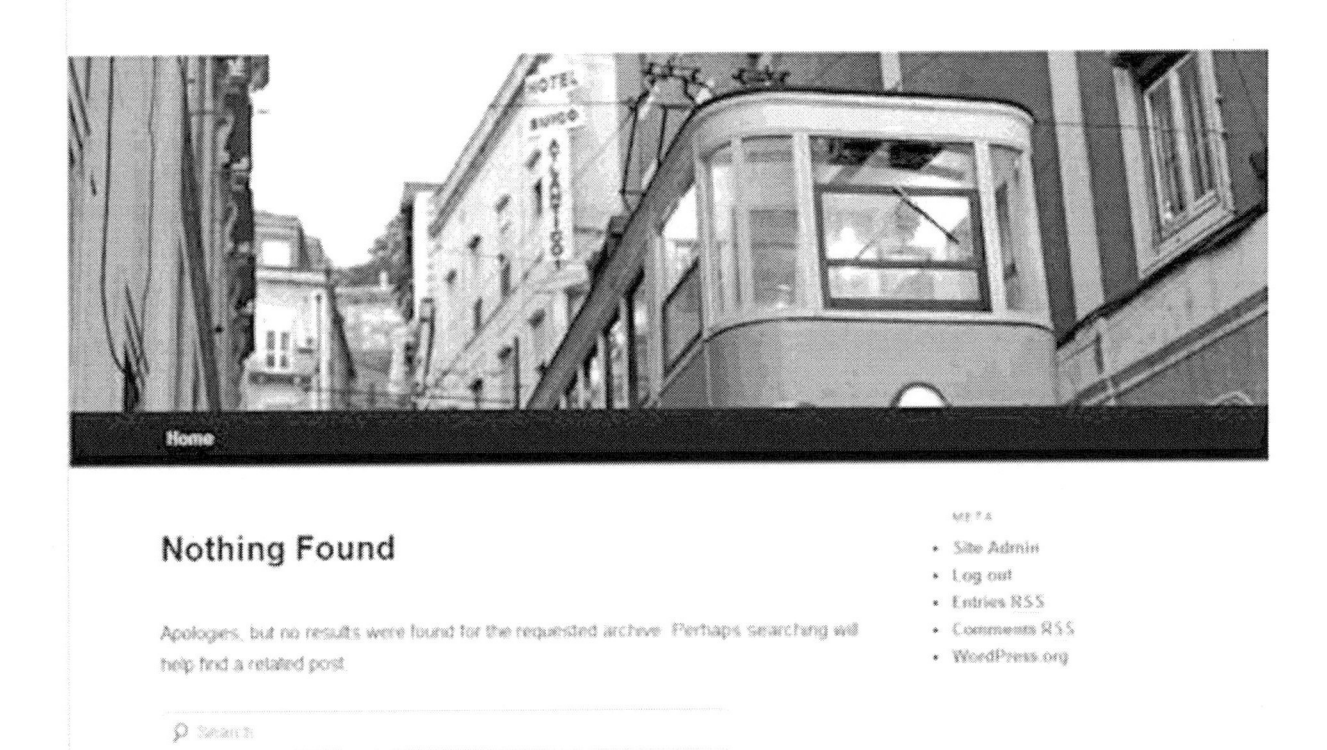

The site will be bare. The homepage will read: "Nothing Found". In my screenshot you can still see the Meta widget I left in the right sidebar.

Before we start configuring WordPress and creating a website, we should take care of any updates that are required.

Tasks to complete

1. Delete the pre-installed Page, Post, Widgets and Comment.

Dashboard updates

WordPress makes it easy for us to know when there are updates. At the top of the screen, you'll see the notification area whenever there is a new update to WordPress itself.

WordPress 3.4.2 is available! Please update now.

. . .

This area doesn't show us when there are updates to plugins but WordPress does have a way to tell us that as well. Whenever there is a plugin to update, WordPress will display a circle with a number inside, right next to the Plugins menu in the sidebar navigation.

NOTE: You'll also see in that screenshot that there are 3 comments waiting to be approved.

In addition to these notification areas, we can find all available updates in the "Updates" section:

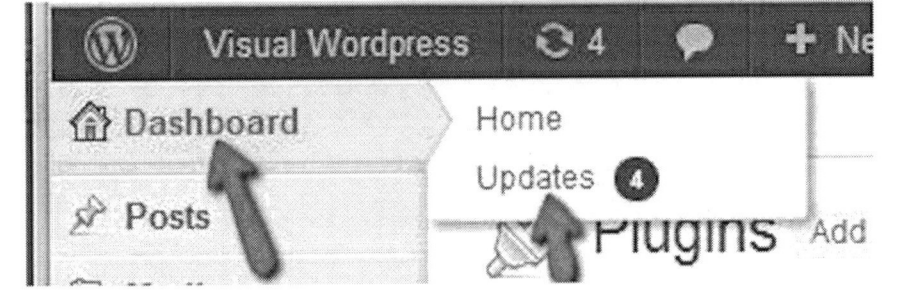

In the above screenshot there are 4 updates I need to take care of.

Click on the Updates menu item to go to the updates screen.

At the top of that screen, there will be a section for WordPress updates (if there is one available):

An updated version of WordPress is available.

You can update to WordPress 3.4.2 automatically or download the package and install it manually.

Update Now   Download 3.4.2

While your site is being updated, it will be in maintenance mode. As soon as your updates are compl

Plugins

To update WordPress to the latest version, simply click the "Update Now" button and follow the onscreen instructions.

Occasionally these WordPress updates will require you to click a button or two, but on this occasion with mine, it went ahead and completed the update all on its own.

After the update, I was taken back to the main Dashboard screen with news of the update and what it fixed/added. However, I need to go back to the updates screen to continue with the other 3 updates.

Plugins

The following plugins have new versions available. Check the ones you want to up

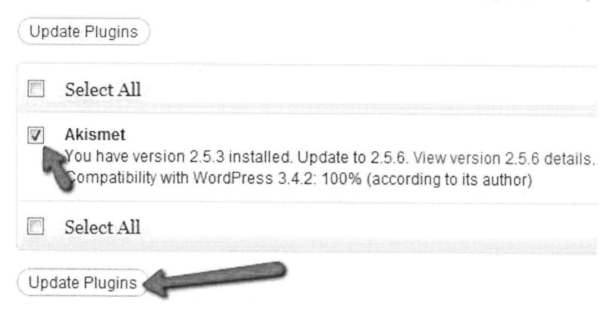

Update Plugins

☐ Select All

☑ **Akismet**
You have version 2.5.3 installed. Update to 2.5.6. View version 2.5.6 details.
Compatibility with WordPress 3.4.2: 100% (according to its author)

☐ Select All

Update Plugins

Simply place a check mark next to all plugins in the list (only one in my screenshot), and click the "Update Plugins" button.

NOTE: If there are multiple plugins to update, click the check box next to the "Select All" text and that will check each one for you and update those that have updates pending.

Once the plugin updates have been completed, WordPress will ask you where you want to go next:

Updating Plugin Akismet (1/1)

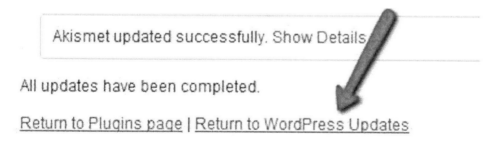

Akismet updated successfully. Show Details

All updates have been completed.

Return to Plugins page | Return to WordPress Updates

If there are still updates to perform, click the link to return to WordPress updates.

The last updates we need to do are for the preinstalled WordPress themes:

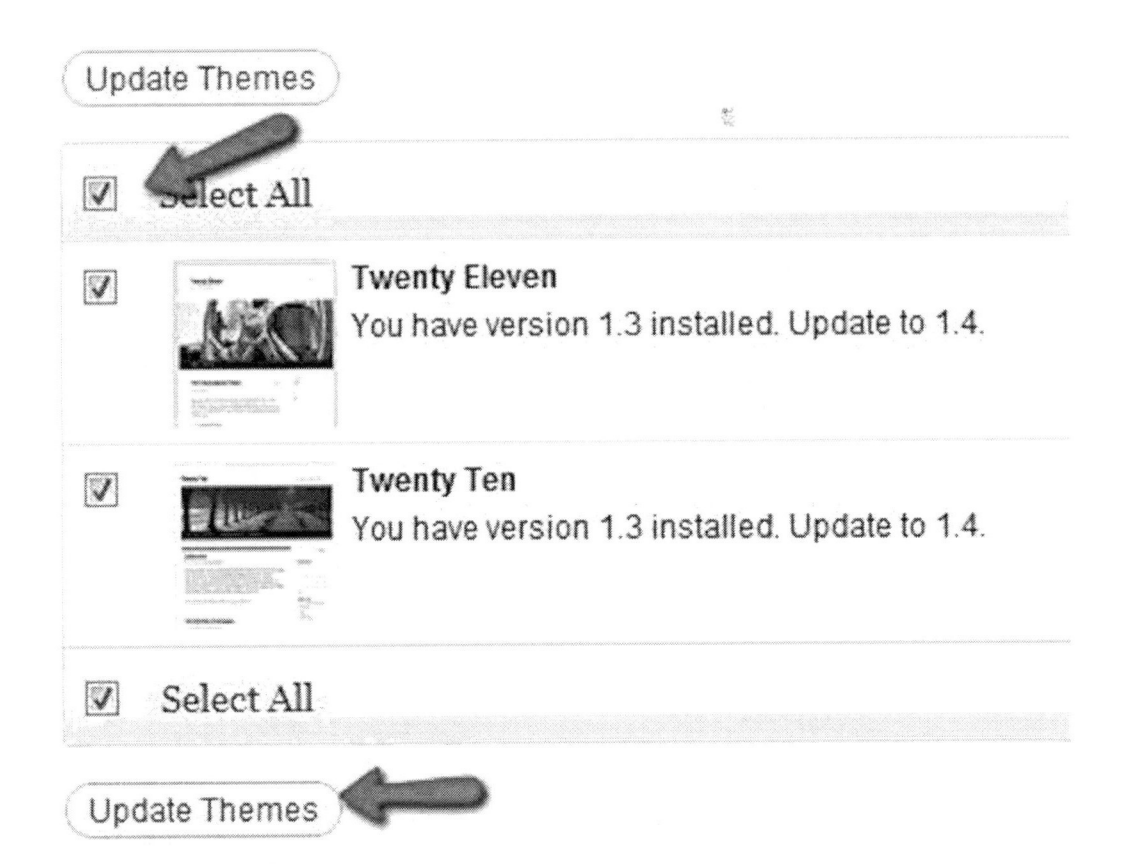

NOTE: We may decide we don't want to use one or both of these themes later on. If that is the case we can delete them now. However, for the moment, let's just update them.

Check the boxes next to both and then click the "Update Themes" button.

The update will proceed and WordPress will again ask you where you want to go when it is finished updating. With all updates now complete, we can actually go anywhere we want by clicking the relevant option in the Dashboard's navigation sidebar.

OK, let's configure WordPress so that it is ready for our content.

Tasks to complete

1. Update WordPress if necessary and any plugins that are out of date.

WordPress Settings

In the sidebar navigation of your Dashboard, you'll see an item labeled "Settings".

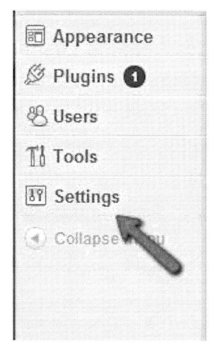

Once again, hovering your mouse over the "Settings" will open a menu.

Settings	General
Collapse menu	Writing
	Reading
	Discussion
	Media
	Permalinks

This "floating" menu is only visible when you move your mouse over the Settings link. If you click directly on the "Settings" link in the sidebar (instead of just hovering the mouse over it), the Settings menu will be expanded directly in the sidebar so all items are visible:

⚙ Settings

General

Writing

Reading

Discussion

Media

Permalinks

You can actually do this with any item in the navigation sidebar that has a sub-menu. Just click the main term to expand the menu directly within the sidebar.

Within Settings we have a number of items. Let's look at each one in turn and configure things as we go through.

General Settings

The General settings page defines some of the basic website settings.

At the top of the screen, the first few settings look like this:

⚙ General Settings

Site Title	Visual Wordpress
Tagline	Learning Wordpress the Visual Way
	In a few words, explain what this site is about.
WordPress Address (URL)	
Site Address (URL)	
	Enter the address here if you want your site homepage to be differe,
E-mail Address	
	This address is used for admin purposes, like new user notification.

The information on the General Settings page was filled in when you installed WordPress, and there is probably no reason to change anything.

Right at the top is the Site Title. This is usually the same as the domain name.

Under the title is the Tagline. On some themes the tagline is displayed in the site header right under the site name. You typically use the tagline to give your visitors a little bit more information about your website. A tagline may be your website's "catch phrase", slogan, mission statement, or just a very brief, one sentence description.

You can see the tagline on the default WordPress theme under the title:

The next two fields on this settings page are the **WordPress Address (URL)** and the **Site Address (URL)**. The WordPress Address is the URL where WordPress is installed. Since we installed it in the root folder of this site, the WordPress Address is identical to the Website Address.

NOTE: Advanced users might want to install WordPress in a folder on their site, yet still have the WordPress site appear as if it were in the root folder. They can achieve this by using the WordPress Address (URL) field. Confused? Don't be. You won't be doing this.

Next on this setting page is the email address. This is very important as you'll get all notifications sent to this email address. Make sure you use a valid email that you actually check frequently. Later in the book we'll assign a Gravatar to this email address and set up a backup system that sends you an email backup of your WordPress database at set intervals.

Lower down this General Setting page are some more options:

Membership	☐ Anyone can register
New User Default Role	Subscriber [v]
Timezone	UTC+0 [v] *UTC time is 2013-(* *Choose a city in the same timezone as you.*
Date Format	⦿ June 28, 2013 ○ 2013/06/28 ○ 06/28/2013 ○ 28/06/2013 ○ Custom: F j, Y June 28, 2013 Documentation on date and time formatting.
Time Format	⦿ 8:03 am ○ 8:03 AM ○ 08:03 ○ Custom: g:i a 8:03 am
Week Starts On	Monday [v]

Save Changes

We can ignore the **Membership** and **New User Default Role** since we are not setting up a site where visitors can register and contribute content.

The rest of the settings on this page allow you to set your time zone, date and time formats.

The time zone is used to correctly timestamp posts on your site. Since we'll look at how you can also schedule your posts into the future, the correct time zone will ensure your posts are going out at the intended dates and times.

Select the date and time format you use.

You can also set the day you use for the start of the week. This will be used if you use a calendar widget in your sidebar (more on widgets later). If you choose Monday as the start of the week, then Monday will be the first column in the calendar.

If you make any changes to the settings on the General Settings tab, make sure you save the changes when you are finished.

Writing

The writing settings control the user interface you see when you are adding/editing posts. Let's look at the options.

Here are the first few:

Formatting has two options. The first one will automatically convert text based emoticons (keyboard characters used to represent facial expressions), to graphic versions. The second option will try to correct any badly nested XHTML. I'd leave these set at the defaults.

The final option, **Default Post Format**, is the default appearance of the posts you add to your site. This is controlled by the template you are using, with different templates having different options. Here are some of those options:

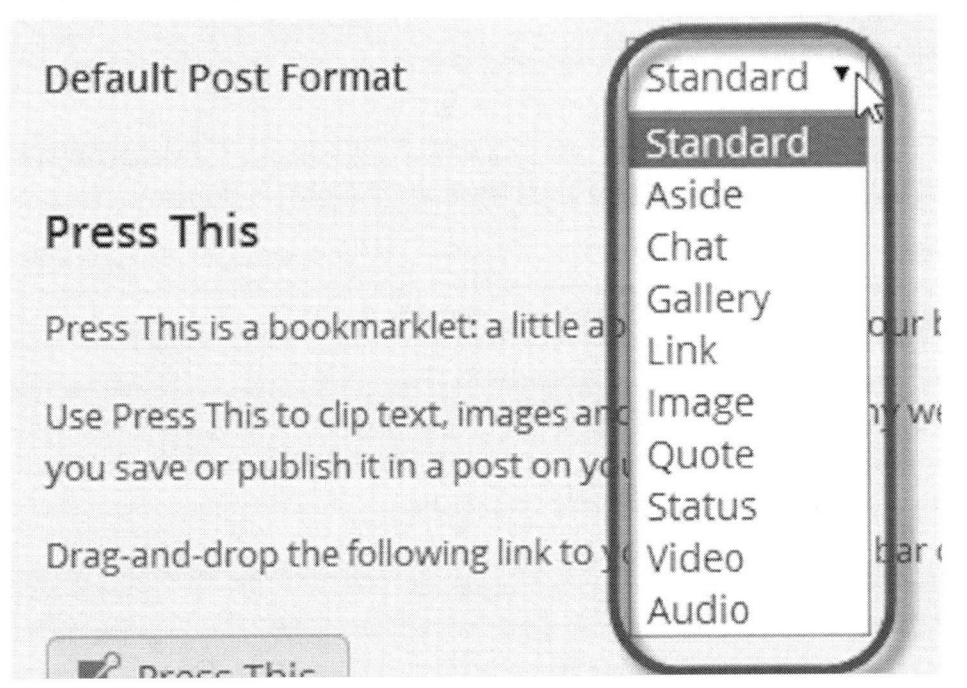

Each of these will modify how the posts look, so I recommend you use the Standard option for the default value, and then change the format on a post by post basis if needed. We'll see how to do that later.

"Press This" is something that most people don't use. However, I will show you how it works and what it is for.

Essentially this is an easy way to add content to your site. Imagine you are on another website, reading a fantastic article and you decide you'd like to mention this article on your own site. The "PressThis bookmarklet" gives us a quick way of doing that.

To use the Bookmarklet, click and drag the Press This button in your WordPress Dashboard up to the bookmarks bar of your web browser and drop it there. Here it is in my own browser:

Let's see what happens when I am on a site that I want to talk about on my own site.

After navigating to a site that I found very interesting, I clicked the Press This button in my bookmark bar:

A window opens with the title of the post already filled in (using the title of the page I want to talk about), plus a link to the post in the main post editor. I can add my own commentary to the post and the link will credit the source of the information.

When you have finished adding your own commentary about why you found the page so interesting, or why your visitors should go and read it, click the **Publish** button to add the post to your own site.

Here are the next few settings:

Post via e-mail

To post to WordPress by e-mail you must set up a secret e-mail account with POP3 access. Any mail received at this address will be posted, so it's a good idea to keep this address very secret. Here are three random strings you could use: 1BZ2M2o6 , sQr2mdep , xk4ZYOCZ .

Mail Server	mail.example.com	Port 110
Login Name	login@example.com	
Password	password	
Default Mail Category	Uncategorized	

The Post via e-mail can be set up so that you can post content to your site by sending it in an email. This is beyond the scope of this book.

The final setting on this page IS important. It's the update services:

Update Services

When you publish a new post, WordPress automatically n
multiple service URLs with line breaks.

http://rpc.pingomatic.com/

Save Changes

Basically, every time you post new content to your site, a message is sent to any service in this list (currently just one). This helps get your content noticed by, and included in, the search engines a lot faster. WordPress installs just one service, but I recommend you add more.

Do a search of Google for "WordPress Ping List" and you'll find people have created lists of services you can add. Just find a list and paste it into the box. Save your changes before moving to the next settings page.

Reading

The reading settings define how your visitors will see certain aspects of your site. There are only a few settings here, but they are important.

Reading Settings

Front page displays
- ○ Your latest posts
- ● A static page (select below)
  - Front page: What Is Curcumin? ▾
  - Posts page: — Select — ▾

Blog pages show at most   10 ▴▾ posts

Syndication feeds show the most recent   10 ▴▾ items

For each article in a feed, show
- ● Full text
- ○ Summary

Search Engine Visibility   ☐ Discourage search engines from indexing this site
It is up to search engines to honor this request.

Save Changes

NOTE: The options surrounded by the red box will only appear if you have a WordPress Page created. Since we deleted the sample page, you won't see this yet. However, this option is very important because it defines what content appears on your website homepage. We'll look at this again later.

The default setting is **Your Latest Post**. This will display the most recent posts on your homepage. The number of posts displayed on your homepage is determined by whatever you have the **Blog pages show at most** set to. Since the default is 10, that means your last 10 posts will appear on your homepage.

However, it is possible to set up the homepage like a more traditional website, with a single article forming the basis of the homepage content. You can do this in WordPress by creating a WordPress PAGE that contains your homepage article. You then select **A Static Page** from the options and choose the page from the **Front Page** drop down list. We'll do this later.

Blog pages show at most, defines how many posts appear on a page. We mentioned this above in relation to the homepage.

This setting will make more sense when you start adding content to your site. You'll then be able to see what WordPress does with that content as you add it. It's not just the homepage that this setting affects.

If you have a category on your site called "types of roses", then WordPress will create a category page called "Types of Roses" that lists all of the articles in that category. If you have 15 articles, each describing a different rose, then WordPress will create two category pages to hold those articles. The first category page will have links to the first 10, and the second will list the remaining 5.

There are other cases where WordPress collects articles together to display on a page, but we'll look at those later in the book. For now though, just realize that this setting defines how many articles WordPress puts onto a single page. I recommend you leave the setting at the default 10.

Syndication feeds show the most recent, refers to your website's RSS feed. Every WordPress site has an RSS feed (in fact it has many RSS feeds). An RSS feed is just a list of the most recent articles with a link and a description for each post. This particular setting allows you to define how many of your most recent posts appear in the feed. Again, I recommend 10. We'll look at RSS feeds in more detail later on.

For each article in a feed, show, defines what content is shown in the feed. If you select "Full Text", then the complete articles are included in the feed. This can make your feed very long, but also give spammers a chance to steal your content with tools designed to scrape RSS feeds and post the content to their own sites.

I recommend you change this setting to Summary. That way only a short summary of each post will be displayed in the feed, which is far less appealing to spammers and easier on the eye for those who genuinely follow your active RSS feeds.

Search Engine Visibility allows you to effectively turn off the site from the search engines. If you are working on a site that you don't yet want the search engines to spider and index, you can check this box.

I actually allow search engines to visit and index my site from day 1. Yes, the search engines will find content that is not finished, but that's OK because they'll come back and check the site periodically to pick up changes.

Whether you block the search engines now or not is up to you. Just remember that if you do, your site won't start appearing in the search engines until you unblock them.

I recommend you leave this setting unchecked.

Discussion

The discussion settings are related to comments that visitors may leave at the end of your posts. There are a few settings we need to change from the default.

Here are the first few settings in the discussion options:

Default article settings

- ☑ Attempt to notify any blogs linked to from the article
- ☑ Allow link notifications from other blogs (pingbacks and trackbacks)
- ☑ Allow people to post comments on new articles

(These settings may be overridden for individual articles.)

Attempt to notify any blogs linked to from the article should be left checked. Whenever you write an article and link to another site, WordPress will try to notify that site that you have linked to them. WordPress does this by sending what is called a Ping. Pings will show up in the comment system of the receiving blog and can be approved like a comment. If it is approved, that Pingback will appear near the comments section on that blog, giving you a link back to your site.

NOTE: Any website can turn pingbacks off. If a ping is sent to a site where pingbacks are OFF, then it won't appear in their comment system.

Here are some example pingbacks published on a web page:

3 Responses to *Men's Health Week Proclamations*

1. Pingback: health » Blog Archive » Focus on Men's Health Week This Father's Day : Healthymagination

2. Pingback: Focus on Men's Health Week This Father's Day : Healthymagination – health

3. Pingback: Focus on Men's Health Week This Father's Day : Healthymagination – men health

Each pingback is a link back to a website that has linked to this webpage.

The next option - **Allow link notifications from other blogs (pingbacks and trackbacks)** allows you to turn pingbacks and trackbacks (trackbacks are very similar to pingbacks) off. If you uncheck this, you will not receive pingbacks or trackbacks.

Should you check it or not?

Well, it's always nice to see when a site is linking to your content. However, there is a technique used by spammers to send fake trackbacks & pingbacks to your site. They are trying to get you to approve their trackback so that your site will then link to theirs.

Personally I leave this options checked (so I can see any new links to my site), but I never approve a trackback or pingback.

Allow people to post comments on new articles should remain checked. It is important that you let your visitors comment on your site's content. A lot of people disable this because they think moderating comments it too much work. However, we'll look at a plugin later that will cut back on spam, which helps a lot with this. Besides, the benefits of having a dialog with your visitors far outweigh the negatives.

The next section of options is shown below:

Other comment settings
- ☑ Comment author must fill out name and e-mail
- ☐ Users must be registered and logged in to comment
- ☐ Automatically close comments on articles older than 14 days
- ☑ Enable threaded (nested) comments 5 levels deep
- ☐ Break comments into pages with 50 top level comments per page and the last page displayed by default
- Comments should be displayed with the older comments at the top of each page

Leave all of these at their default value (shown above).

The options are fairly self-explanatory.

The second item should remain unchecked, because we do not allow visitors to register and login to our site. We do want *all* visitors to have the option of leaving a comment though.

The third option allows you to close the comment sections on posts after a certain number of days. I like to leave comments open indefinitely as you never know when someone will find your article and want to have their say.

Nested comments should be enabled. This allows people to engage in discussions within the comments section, with replies to previous comments appearing "nested" underneath the comment they are replying to. Here is an example showing how nested comments appear on my site:

> **Marshall says:**
> 18/6/2013 at 05:06
>
> I purchased the KD Suite tonight because Andy does good videos. I could have purchased directly from Guindon since I had purchased other products from him. However the productpay.com fulfillment system absolutely sucks. I did not get my bonus downloads because the bonus page got closed before I could get all the membership BS set up and then back to the download page. As opposed to other systems such as JVZoo where you get download information and login information from them, productpay sucks your money and does not much else. And they have no way to contact them without setting up another account with them just to send a support ticket. Plus they hide behind Domains by Proxy owned by Godaddy.com. What kind of legitimate fulfillment company needs to hide their registration information. I have contacted Guindon directly about this and I am sure Dave will make it right. But what a pain in the butt process. If you purchase from productpay.com just be forwarned to download everything first then worry about any membership BS.
>
> You can bet none of Dr Andy's membership sites worked like this. I know because I bought a lot of his products.
>
> Reply
>
>> **Andy Williams says:**
>> 18/6/2013 at 07:59
>>
>> Totally agree Marshall. They really could do a lot better. Also, thanks for your loyalty 😊
>>
>> Reply
>>
>>> **Marshall says:**
>>> 18/6/2013 at 09:56
>>>
>>> Andy You are welcome. Your software has always worked out of the box without a lot of bugs. And the very few that came up you fixed right away. Your courses were right on the mark too. For what it is worth, Dave got about 5 emails from me tonight so maybe he will rethink his choice of fulfillment companies.
>>>
>>> The KD Bestseller analyzer was worth the hassle of getting it and getting it activated. I have played with it for about 3 hours tonight. My niche I was writing in is a real loser for making money. The fiction, adventure, romance are really hot now. I have one more herb book to do

You can see that replies to the previous comment are nested underneath them, making it clear that the comments are part of a conversation.

The last two options in this section relate to how comments are displayed on the page. If you want, comments can be spread across multiple pages, with say 50 comments per page (default). However, I leave this option unchecked so that all comments for an article appear on the same page. If you find that you get hundreds of comments per article, you might like to enable this option just so pages load a lot quicker.

The final option in this section allows you to show older or newer comments at the top of the comments section.

I prefer to have comments listed in the order in which they are submitted as that makes more sense. Therefore leave the setting as "older".

The next section of these settings is shown below:

The first two options will send you an email whenever someone posts a comment, and when a comment is held for moderation. We'll actually set up comments so that ALL comments must be moderated so the second option is less important.

Leave both of the first two options checked so that you know when someone leaves a comment. When you get an email notification, you can then login to your Dashboard and either approve the comment (so it goes live on your site), or send it to trash if it's blatant spam.

The second two options shown above relate to when a comment can appear on the site. Check the box next to **Comment must be manually approved**. This will mean ALL comments must be approved by you. We don't want spammy comments appearing on the site and since they'll only appear when we approve them, we have 100% control.

Since we are now moderating all comments, the **Comment author must have a previously approved comment** becomes less important. What this setting can do is auto-approve comments for any author that has a previously approved comment on the site. For this to work, the previous option should remain unchecked. However, I don't advise this. Set up your settings as I have them in the screenshot above.

The next setting is not important to us since all our comments are moderated.

Comment Moderation

Hold a comment in the queue if it contains 2 ☐ or more links. (A common characteristic of comment spam is a large number of hyperlinks.)

When a comment contains any of these words in its content, name, URL, e-mail, or IP, it will be held in the moderation queue. One word or IP per line. It will match inside words, so "press" will match "WordPress".

If you do not have it set up to moderate all comments, you can use this setting to automatically add comments to the moderation queue IF it has a certain number of links in it (default is 2), OR the comment contains a word that is listed in the big box.

Since all of our comments are moderated anyway, we can leave this section as it is.

The Comment Blacklist box allows you to set up a blacklist to automatically reject comments that meet the criteria listed here.

Comment Blacklist

When a comment contains any of these words in its content, name, URL, e-mail, or IP, it will be marked as spam. One word or IP per line. It will match inside words, so "press" will match "WordPress".

Essentially any comment that contains a word listed in this box, contains a URL listed in this box, comes from an email address listed in this box, or comes from an IP address listed in this box, will automatically be sent to the comment spam folder.

That means you can set up your blacklist with "unsavory" words, email addresses, URLs or IP addresses of known spammers, and you'll never see those comments in your moderation queue. The comment blacklist can significantly cut down on your comment moderation, so I suggest you do a search on Google for **WordPress comment blacklist**, and use a list that someone else has already put together (you'll find a few). Just copy and paste their list into the box and save the settings.

The final section of the discussion options is related to Avatars:

Avatars

An avatar is an image that follows you from weblog to weblog appearing beside your name when you comment on avatar enabled sites. Here you can enable the display of avatars for people who comment on your site.

Avatar Display	☑ Show Avatars
Maximum Rating	◉ G — Suitable for all audiences
	○ PG — Possibly offensive, usually for audiences 13 and above
	○ R — Intended for adult audiences above 17
	○ X — Even more mature than above
Default Avatar	For users without a custom avatar of their own, you can either display a generic logo or a generated one based on their e-mail address.

○ Mystery Man

◉ Blank

○ Gravatar Logo

○ Identicon (Generated)

○ Wavatar (Generated)

○ MonsterID (Generated)

○ Retro (Generated)

Save Changes ⟵

An Avatar is a little graphic that appears next to the commenter's name.

I think it is nice to see who is leaving comments, so I recommend you leave Avatars on (first setting).

For most websites you should have the maximum rating set to G. Avatars are assigned ratings when you create them over at Gravatar.com, so this ratings system is only as good as the honesty of the person creating the avatar.

The final setting allows you to define the default action if someone does not have an Avatar set up for their email address. In the screenshot above, I still have it set to **Mystery Man** but I recommend you select **Blank** so that no avatar is shown. This is because Avatar images need to load with the page. Any page with a lot of comments will have a lot of Avatars to load and this slows down the load speed of the page. Why slow it further with "Mystery Man" avatars when the commenter doesn't have an avatar set up?

When you have finished with these settings, save the changes you made.

Media

The media settings relate to images and other media that you might insert into your site.

Image sizes

The sizes listed below determine the maximum dimensions in pixels to use when inserting an image into the body of a post.

Thumbnail size

Width 150 ⬍ Height 150 ⬍

☑ Crop thumbnail to exact dimensions (normally thumbnails are proportional)

Medium size

Max Width 300 ⬍ Max Height 300 ⬍

Large size

Max Width 1024 ⬍ Max Height 1024 ⬍

These first few settings allow you define the maximum dimensions for thumbnail, medium and large images. You can leave these are the default setting.

The final option asks whether you want your images organized into month and year based folders.

Uploading Files

☑ Organize my uploads into month- and year-based folders

[Save Changes]

I'd recommend you leave this checked, just so your images are organized into dates on your server. It can help you find the images later if you need to.

Permalinks

The final settings are the permalinks. Basically these define how the URLs (web address), are constructed for content on your site. This needs to be changed from the default value.

We want the URLs on our site to help visitors and search engines, so we'll add in the post's category and name to the URL:

Common Settings

○ Default	http:/ ▓▓▓▓▓ .com/?p=123
○ Day and name	http:/ ▓▓▓▓▓ .com/2013/06/28/sample-post/
○ Month and name	http:/ ▓▓▓▓▓ .com/2013/06/sample-post/
○ Numeric	http:/ ▓▓▓▓▓ .com/archives/123
○ Post name	http:/ ▓▓▓▓▓ .com/sample-post/
● Custom Structure	http:/ ▓▓▓▓▓ .com `/%category%/%postname%/`

Select the **Custom Structure** radio button at the bottom of the list, and enter the following into the box:

/%category%/%postname%/

Save the changes.

The URLs on your site will now look like this:

http://mydomain/category/post-name

The last two options on this settings page are shown below:

Optional

If you like, you may enter custom structures for your category and tag URLs here. For example, using `topics` as your category base would make your category links like `http://example.org/topics/uncategorized/` . If you leave these blank the defaults will be used.

Category base	
Tag base	

[Save Changes]

I would leave these two boxes empty.

When WordPress creates a category page or a tag page, the URL will include the word "category" or "tag".

For example:

http://mydomain.com/**category**/roses/

.. might be the URL of a category page listing my posts on Roses, and

http://mydomain.com/**tag**/red

.. might be a tag page listing all posts on my site that were tagged with the word "red".

If you enter a word into the category base or tag base, when the URLs are constructed, they'll contain the category base or tag base you specified, rather than the default words, "category" or "tag".

Having keywords in your URL can be helpful, BUT, with Google on the warpath of web spammers, I would not even consider entering a category base or tag base. Leave those boxes empty.

Congratulations, you have now set up your main WordPress Settings.

Tasks to complete

1. Go through each of the menus inside the settings menu and make the changes described in this chapter.

RSS feeds

We mentioned RSS feeds earlier when setting up the Reading options.

RSS feeds are an important part of your WordPress website, so I wanted to spend a little more time on this.

RSS stands for **R**eally **S**imple **S**yndication (or **R**ich **S**ite Summary). An RSS feed lists information about the most recent posts on your site. This information is typically the title of the post (which links to the article on your website), and a description of it, which can be short or the entire piece.

The RSS feed is an XML document that would be difficult to read without special software, but XML is the perfect "language" to store this particular type of information.

Most web browsers can read RSS feeds and show its content as readable text. Here is an RSS feed from a websites on "juicing", as displayed in Google Chrome:

Current Feed Content

Measuring heat with the Scoville Scale
Posted: Fri, 12 Oct 2012 18:20:17 +0000

Chili heat is measured on the Scoville scale.

The World's Hottest Chili
Posted: Thu, 11 Oct 2012 15:01:00 +0000

What happens when you eat the world's hottest chili pepper? Watch this video and find out

Health benefits of the Jalapeno Chili pepper
Posted: Thu, 11 Oct 2012 10:32:57 +0000

I love tabasco sauce. There is something about the spicy taste that is addictive. Since I found out about the health benefits of capsaicin in chilies, I have been enjoying even more tabasco and started growing my own chilies.

Antioxidant 2011 Championships
Posted: Mon, 08 Oct 2012 21:11:00 +0000

Some interesting experiments with Asotaxanthin. The second experiment with egg yolks is quite incredible

You can see the summaries of the last 4 posts on my site.

Each entry has the title of the post which is hyperlinked to the article on my site. Under the title is the date and time of the post and then a short description under that.

This is much easier for humans to read than the raw XML code. Here is the raw XML for just the first item in that RSS feed:

54

```
<feedburner:feedburnerHostname xmlns:feedburner="
http://rssnamespace.org/feedburner/ext/1.0">http://feedburner.google.com
</feedburner:feedburnerHostname>
<item>
    <title>Anti-inflammatory juice</title>
    <link>http://juicingtherainbow.com/2380/recipes/anti-inflammatory-juice/</link>
    <comments>
    http://juicingtherainbow.com/2380/recipes/anti-inflammatory-juice/#comments
    </comments>
    <pubDate>Fri, 14 Jun 2013 09:42:46 +0000</pubDate>
    <dc:creator>Andy Williams</dc:creator>
    <category><![CDATA[Recipes]]></category>
    <guid isPermaLink="false">http://juicingtherainbow.com/?p=2380</guid>
    <description><![CDATA[Inflammation is one of the main causes of disease, and a
    lot of the foods we eat contribute to the inflammation.  With chronic
    inflammation comes disease.  This juice is a powerful anti-inflammatory drink,
    and it's tasty too.]]></description>
    <wfw:commentRss>
    http://juicingtherainbow.com/2380/recipes/anti-inflammatory-juice/feed/
    </wfw:commentRss>
    <slash:comments>0</slash:comments>
</item>
<item>
    <title>Carrot pulp salad</title>
    <link>http://juicingtherainbow.com/2320/recipes/carrot-pulp-salad/</link>
    <comments>http://juicingtherainbow.com/2320/recipes/carrot-pulp-salad/#comments
```

Every post in the RSS feed has an entry like this.

RSS feeds provide an easy way for people to follow information they are interested in.

For example, if someone was interested in juicing, they could take the RSS feed from their favorite juicing websites and then add them to an RSS reader, like the free Feedly.com for example.

Using a tool like Feedly, you can follow dozens of RSS feeds of interest. RSS used this way allows you to scan hundreds of articles by title and description, and only click through to read the ones that you are really interested in.

That is why we have RSS feeds on our site.

WordPress has multiple RSS feeds

WordPress has a main RSS feed at **mydomain.com/feed**. Type that into your web browser substituting mydomain.com for your real domain name, and you'll see yours. However, WordPress also creates a lot of other RSS feeds.

For example, an RSS feed is created for each category of posts on your site. If you have a category called "roses", then there will be an RSS feed showing just the posts in the roses category.

To find the URL of any feed, simply go to the category page on the site and add **feed** to the end of it, like this:

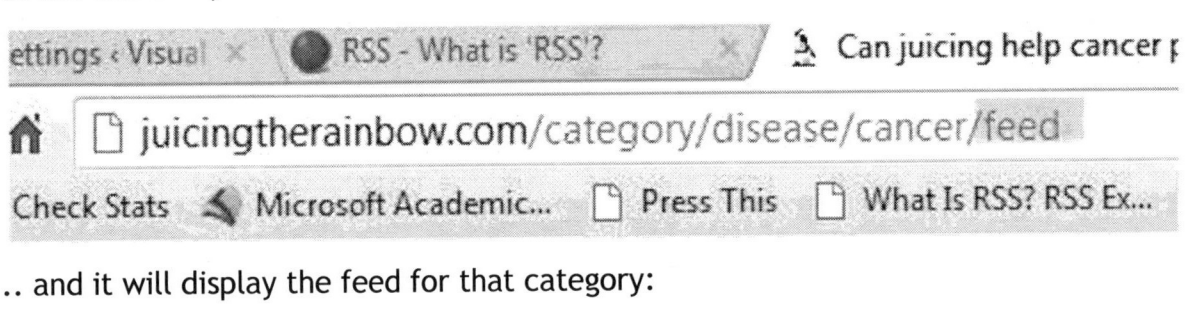

.. and it will display the feed for that category:

Juicing The Rainbow » Cancer [+add to my feedly]

Be the first follower (served in 322ms)

FEB 01 2012

Carcinoid Tumors
Carcinoid tumors grow slowly and affect the gastrointestinal tract and lungs. While juice therapy is not recommended for this type of cancer, there are juices you should avoid.
Juicing the Rainbow » Cancer / by Andy Williams / 512d

Cancer of the Stomach
Sufferers of stomach cancer often have problems with getting enough nutrients in their diet. We take a brief look at the fruit and vegetables that may help.
Juicing the Rainbow » Cancer / by Andy Williams / 512d

Cancer of the Ovaries
Ovarian cancer doesn't often provide strong symptoms. Juicing can help provide support from this type of cancer, but only ONE type of juice.
Juicing the Rainbow » Cancer / by Andy Williams / 512d

NOTE: The feed in the screenshot above is being displayed by a Google Chrome plugin called Feedly News Reader. If you use Google Chrome, you can find this plugin in the Chrome web store (it's totally free):

https://chrome.google.com/webstore

Other RSS feeds created by WordPress include RSS feeds for tag pages, author pages, comments, search results, and so on. You can read more about WordPress RSS feeds here if you're interested:

http://codex.wordpress.org/WordPress_Feeds

RSS feeds can help our pages get indexed

Since RSS feeds link back to our website, we can get some backlinks to our pages, which in turn help them get found by the search engines. The backlinks you get from these RSS feeds are very low quality, so they won't affect your search engine rankings much, but they do help get content indexed quickly, so it is worth submitting your main site feed to an RSS Directory like Feedagg.com.

Search Google for **RSS feed submission** and you'll find more sites you can submit your main feed to. I recommend only submitting it to 3 or 4 of the top RSS feed directories though.

When you next post a new article to your site, the feeds on your site are updated, which in turn updates the feed on Feedagg, which now includes a link back to your new article. The search engines monitor sites like this to find new content, so your new article is found very quickly.

Tasks to complete

1. Go and have a look at Google Reader. If necessary create an account but you can just login with a gmail address if you have one.

2. Subscribe to some feeds that are of interest and look through them to find articles that appeal to you. This will give you a good idea of how feeds can be helpful.

3. At the moment, because you have no content on your site, you won't have any meaningful feeds. However, as soon as you start adding content to your site, find the feed URLs where that content appears (main feed, category feed, tag feed, author feed & search feed).

User Profile

When someone comes to your website, they often want to see who is behind the information. Your user profile in WordPress allows you to tell your visitors a little bit about yourself.

In the Dashboard, hover your mouse over the **Users** link in the navigation menu and then select **Your Profile**.

Your user profile should then load. If you see a list of users instead of the profile, it means you clicked the **Users** link, so just click on your username to get to your profile.

At the top of the Profile screen you'll see a couple of settings:

The top box should be left unchecked as we want the visual editor to be displayed when we are writing content. We'll cover that later in the book.

The Admin color scheme - choose whichever you prefer. As you check an option, your Dashboard color scheme will change to reflect your choice. You may be spending a lot of time in your Dashboard, so choose a color scheme you like.

I don't use keyboard shortcuts for comment moderation, but if you are not a mouse person, then you might like to enable this and follow the "more Information" link to learn how to use it.

What is important on this screen is the **Show Toolbar when viewing site**. We will look at that later, but for now, make sure it is checked.

The next set of Profile options are for your name:

Name

Username	Andy
First Name	Andy
Last Name	Williams
Nickname *(required)*	Andy
Display name publicly as	Andy Williams ▾

Your username cannot be changed. It will be whatever you chose when you installed WordPress.

Enter your real first and last name (or your persona name if you are working with a pen name).

Under nickname you can write anything. I typically use my first name.

The **Display name publicly as** field will be the name used on each page of your web site telling the visitors who wrote the article. Here it is on one of my sites:

You are here: Home / Google Updates / Recent Google Panda & Penguin Updates

Recent Google Panda & Penguin Updates

8/10/2012 BY ANDY WILLIAMS • 19 COMMENTS

It's been a busy couple of weeks at the Google Zoo. Here was their schedule:

September 27th, 2012 – Panda algorithm update.

The Panda algorithm update on the 27th was a fairly major update to the algorithm, and refresh like most previous Panda update.

59

NOTE: If you have a Google Plus account and want to link your content to your Google plus profile, use the same name as your Google plus profile for your display name. Linking your site to your Google plus account is beyond the scope of this book.

The next few options are contact information.

Contact Info

E-mail *(required)*

Website

The only one that is required here is the email address and we have talked earlier about how important that is. If you want to fill out the website field, you can, but this is more useful if you have multiple authors on your site, each with their own personal website.

The last bit of information in your profile is your "bio".

About Yourself

Biographical Info

Here is my short bio

Share a little biographical information to fill out your profile. This may be shown publicly.

New Password

If you would like to change the password type a new one. Otherwise leave this blank.

Type your new password again.

Strength indicator

Hint: The password should be at least seven characters long. To make it stronger, use upper and lower case letters, numbers and symbols like ! " ? $ % ^ &).

I recommend you fill in a short biography as some themes will show this on the author page. Here is the author page on my demo website. It will list all posts I have made on the website:

About Andy Williams

Here is my short bio.

Hello world!

Posted on October 15, 2012

Welcome to WordPress. This is your first post. Edit or delete it, then start blogging! ☺

See how it has pulled in the Bio from my profile page?

Also, note how my photo is included? Let's see how to do that now.

Gravatars

A Gravatar is simply a photograph or image that you can connect to your email address.

Sites that use Gravatar information, like WordPress, will show that image whenever possible, if you contribute something.

For example, your photo will show on your author page. It will also show on any WordPress site where you leave a comment (assuming you use that email address when leaving the comment). Some themes can even show your photo after each post along with your author's bio.

Go over to Gravatar.com.

Fill in your email address in the form and click **Get Your Gravatar**.

You'll be taken to another screen to sign up. Just enter your email again.

Gravatar.com will send an email to your email address. You need to open it and click the confirmation link to activate your new Gravatar account.

On clicking that link, you'll be taken back to a signup screen that asks you for a username and password (twice). Fill these in to create your Gravatar account.

NOTE: You may need to try several usernames as you obviously cannot use one that someone else has taken. If your desired username is taken, then try adding the year of your birth to the end. That usually works for me.

After submitting your registration information, you will then be taken to a screen that allows you to assign a photo to your email address:

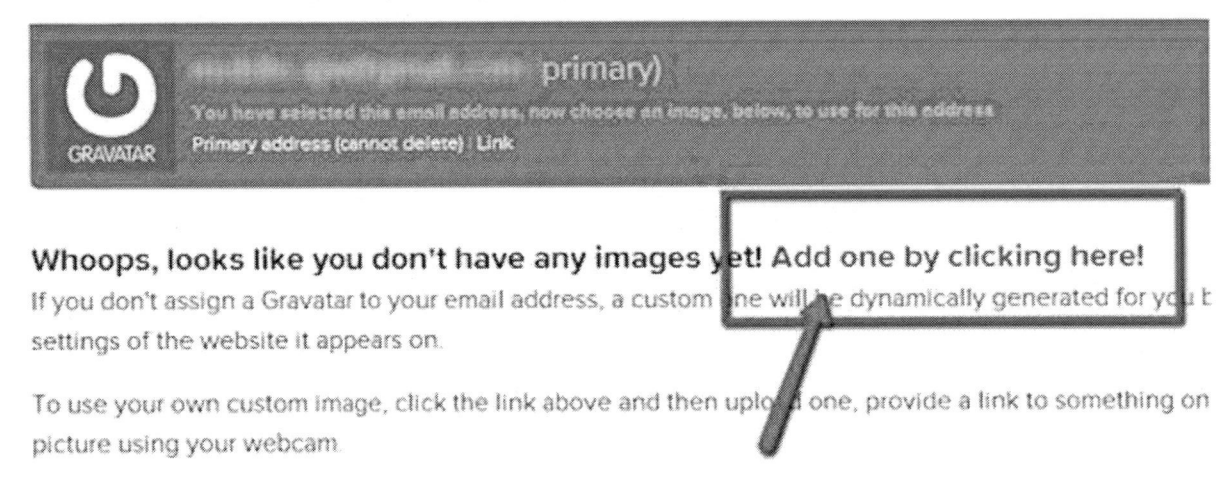

Just click the link and you'll be able to choose an image from a number of different places, including images stored on your hard disk. You'll get an option to crop the image, so don't worry if there is other stuff in the photo that you don't want included. Just crop it out when given the chance.

You now need to rate your image (remember, we mentioned Gravatar ratings earlier when setting up WordPress):

Choose a rating for your Gravatar

By clicking on one of these ratings

rated	rated	rated	rated
G	**PG**	**R**	**X**

Just click the appropriate button.

That's it. Your Gravatar should now be attached to your site's email address. Now, whenever you leave comments on a WordPress site, use that email address and your image will show up along with your comment (assuming they haven't turned Avatars off).

OK, in the next section we'll start to improve the visual aspects of our website by looking at themes, headers and much more.

Tasks to complete

1. Go and claim your Gravatar.
2. Go in and complete you user profile.
3. Find a WordPress site in your niche, and go leave a relevant comment. Watch as your image appears next to your comment.

Tools

The Tools menu has three options:

The Available tools screen offers you "Press This", which we saw earlier in the book. There is also another tool called **Categories and Tag Converter**. This helps make categories into tags and vice versa. This functionality needs to be installed separately as a WordPress plugin. Clicking on the Import link will take you to the Import screen which has a link to that tool's download page. If you want to use it, I suggest you read the instructions on the Plugin's download page.

The Import and Export features allow you to move content from one blog to another. I have used it when I wanted to merge two or more websites into one larger website. Simply export from one WordPress site, and import its data into the one you want to add the content to.

Again, Importing content requires a plugin that you'll get from the Import screen.

To Export Content, click the Export menu:

Export

When you click the button below WordPress will create an XML file for you

This format, which we call WordPress eXtended RSS or WXR, will contain y

Once you've saved the download file, you can use the Import function in a

Choose what to export

◉ All content

This will contain all of your posts, pages, comments, custom fields, terms, navi

○ Posts

○ Pages

○ Views

[Download Export File]

You can then choose what to export. All content, or choose between posts or pages. If you select posts (or pages), you will be given more options including categories to export, export by author, date range or status (published, scheduled, draft, etc).

You will then click the export button to download the export file to your computer.

To Import, install the Import plugin that is linked to from the Import screen:

Import

If you have posts or comments in another system, WordPress can import those into this site. To get s

Blogger	Install the Blogger importer to import posts, comments, an
Blogroll	Install the blogroll importer to import links in OPML format
Categories and Tags Converter	Install the category/tag converter to convert existing catego
LiveJournal	Install the LiveJournal importer to import posts from LiveJo
Movable Type and TypePad	Install the Movable Type importer to import posts and com
RSS	Install the RSS importer to import posts from an RSS feed.
Tumblr	Install the Tumblr importer to import posts & media from T
WordPress	Install the WordPress importer to import posts, pages, com

If the importer you need is not listed, search the plugin directory to see if an importer is available.

Then make sure you activate it. You can now import the file that was previously exported. Just go to the Import screen again, click the link to the WordPress plugin, and you'll see the following screen:

Import WordPress

Howdy! Upload your WordPress eXtended RSS (WXR) file and we'll import the posts, pages, comments, site.

Choose a WXR (.xml) file to upload, then click Upload file and import.

Choose a file from your computer: (Maximum size: 64MB) [Choose File] No file chosen

[Upload file and import]

Choose the file and upload.

Appearance menu

If you click on the Appearance link in the Dashboard Navigation sidebar, it will open up to expose you more menu items:

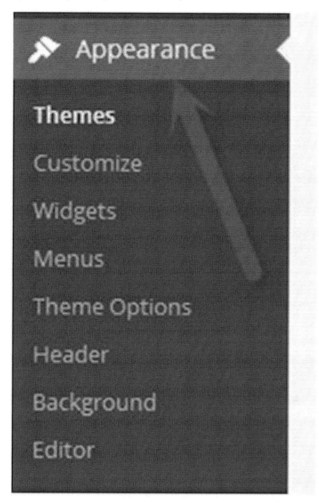

This menu gives you access to settings that control how your website looks. It specifically relates to the template or theme you are using.

Clicking on the Appearance menu actually opens up the themes setting page.

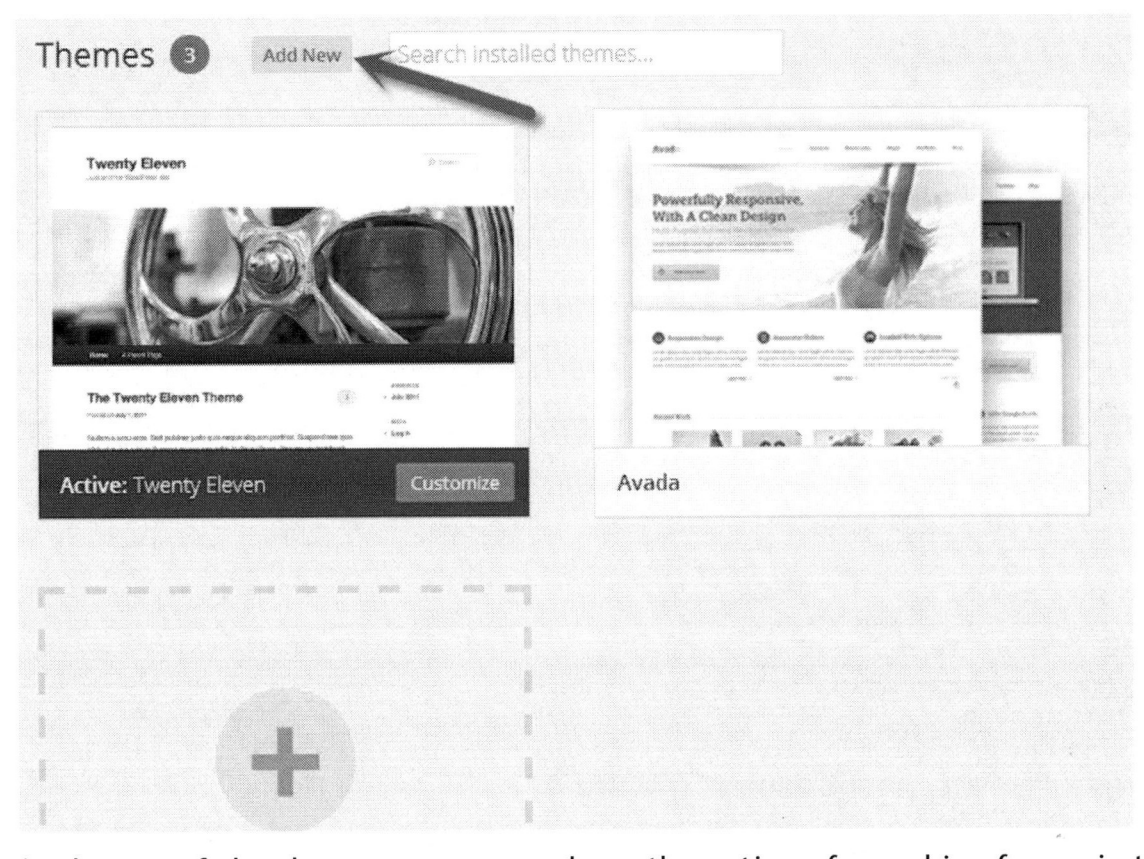

At the top of the themes screen, you have the option of searching for an installed theme (you will only have a couple of installed themes and you can see thumbnails of them all below this top bar) or **Add New** theme, which will search Wordpress approved themes on the internet.

NOTE: You will often hear people referring to WordPress themes as templates. While the two things are not totally the same thing, people often use the words interchangeably to mean the same. So for the purpose of this book, templates and themes are the same thing.

The currently selected theme is shown in the first position, with a **Customize** button next to the text **Active: Twenty Eleven** (or whatever your active theme is called).

The customize button will take you to a WYSIWYG editor allowing you to make some design changes to the appearance of your site.

In this book, we will work with the Twenty Eleven theme to get the look and feel we want for our site.

Click on the customize button to open the editor:

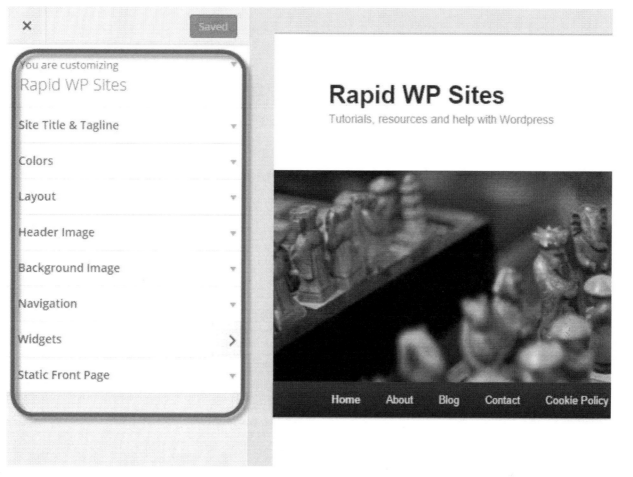

On the left is a menu that gives you access to certain configuration settings. On the right, the large window shows a preview of how your site will appear with the currently selected settings. Make changes and watch the preview update as you design how your site will look and feel.

At the top of the menu is Site Title & Tagline. These options can also be changed in the General Settings we saw earlier (with the exception of one setting).

You can type in the title and tagline and watch the preview display on the right side update with the new settings.

The one setting that is new here is the **Display Header Text** checkbox. If you uncheck this, see what happens to the preview. The Site name and tagline disappear. The search box is also moved from this area down to the black menu bar. Try it.

Why might you want to remove the Site title and tagline?

You might decide to include the title and tagline within the header image instead. By combining the two, you can save space at the top of your theme (which currently shows this information as two separate sections). We'll look later at how you can easily create a custom header graphic containing the Site Title and tagline. You can then come back here and remove the header text from your site by unchecking this box.

The next menu is the colours menu:

At the top you'll see a couple of radio buttons that allow you to switch between two readymade schemes – light and dark. The light scheme is basically dark text on a white background, and the dark scheme is light text on black background. Play around by selecting each one to see how they display in the preview screen.

You can manually change the colours of the header text, background colour, and link colour. I suggest you actually leave these alone because too many colours can ruin a design. Simple is better. If you do want to experiment, click the box under the setting that you wish to change. You can click directly inside the coloured box to open the colour selector.

Header Text Color

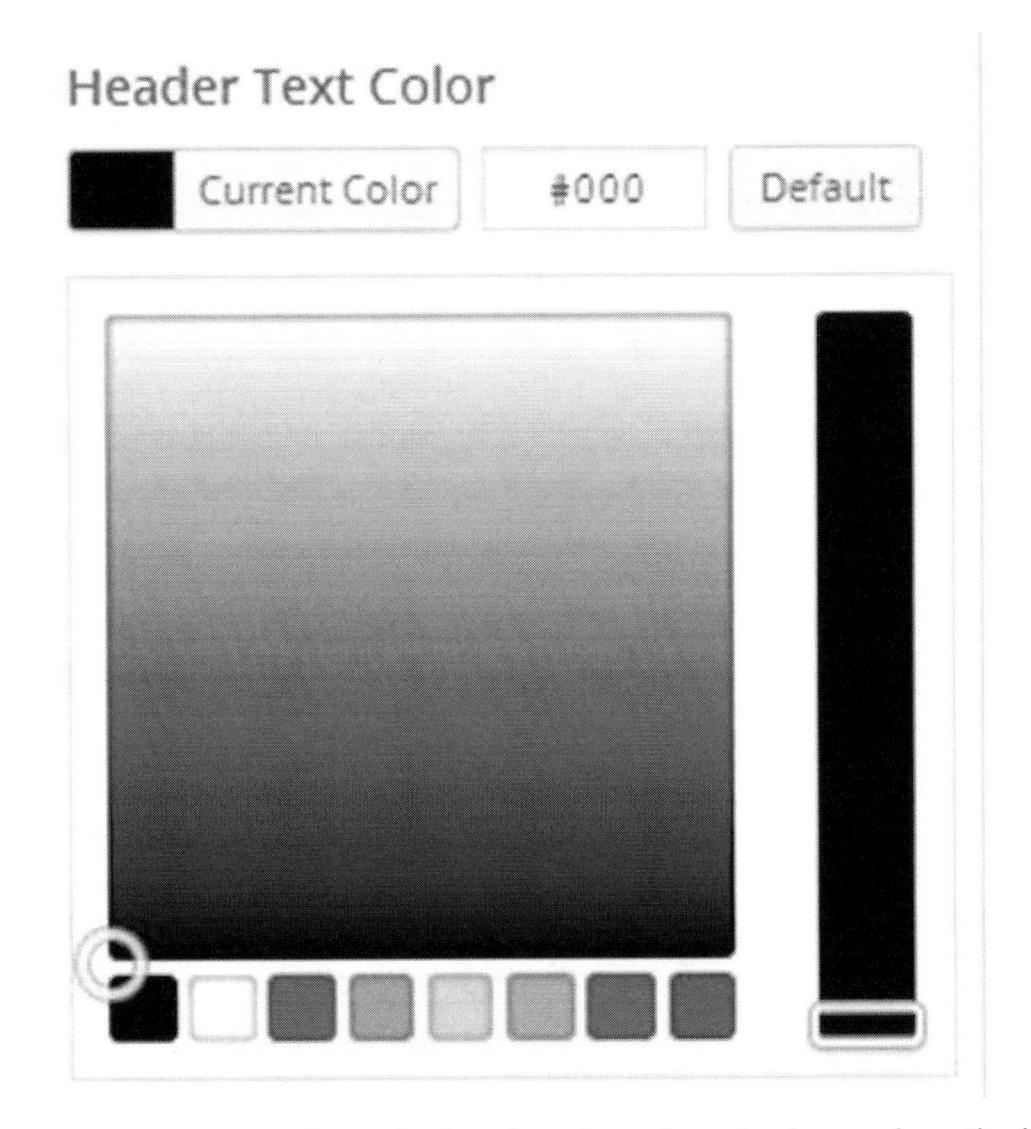

From here, you can select a basic colour from the color boxes along the bottom, and then choose the tone of that colour using the large central square. You can also lighten or darken your selected color using the vertical bar on the right.

The next menu is the layout menu.

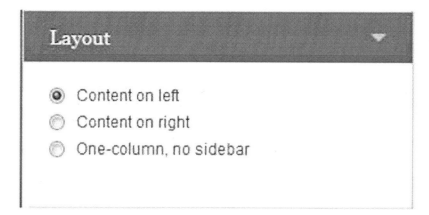

This allows you to select which side of your webpage the menu is located. If you select **Content on left**, the menu will be on the right. **Content on right** leaves the menu on the left. You can also choose to have no sidebar if that's what you want. I don't recommend a **one-column, no sidebar** layout for a multipage site though, as the sidebar is an important area for adding navigation, monetization, promotional stuff, and so on.

The settings you choose will be your personal preference. I prefer my sidebar on the right (content left).

The next menu is the header image.

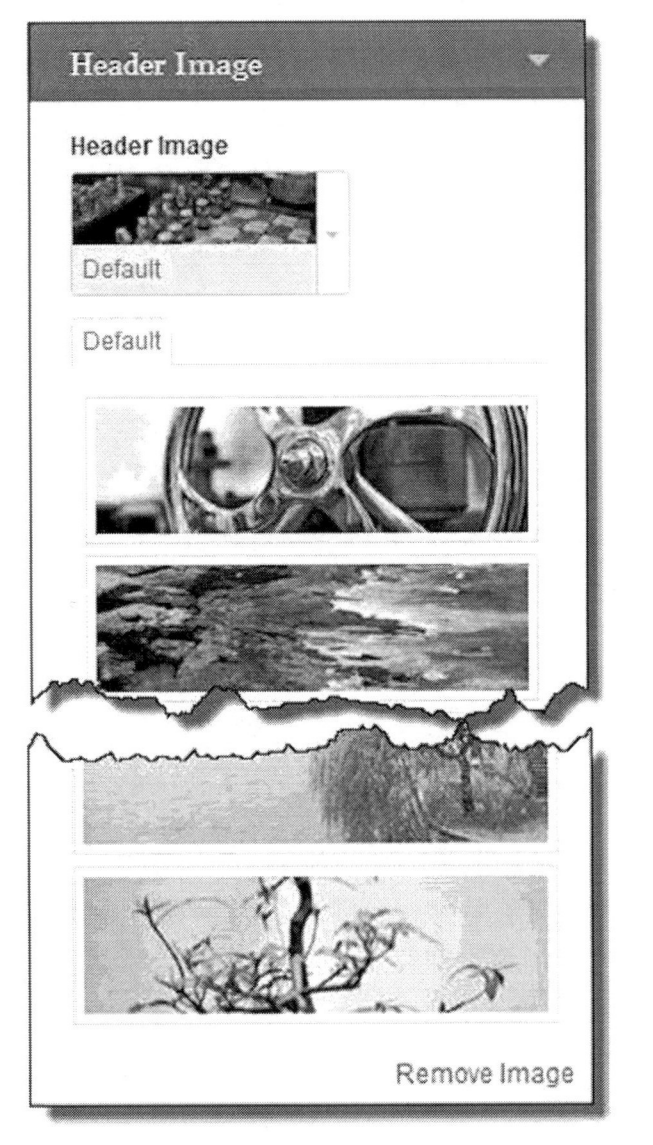

I have cut out part of the middle section as it just lists lots of default header images. If you like one, select it and see how the preview changes. Later in the book we will replace this header with our own unique custom image.

At the bottom, there is also a link to **Remove Image**. This will take the image off your site and just leave the Title and Tagline in the header area. Try it! You can easily add it back if you want to by clicking on one of the images.

The next option is the Background image.

Background Image

Background Image

No Image ▾

Upload New

Drop a file here or select a file.

You can drag and drop an image from your computer into the dashed box above and it will upload to your site as a background image. Go ahead and try it now.

When the image is uploaded, more options become available to you:

Upload New | Uploaded

Drop a file here or select a file.

Remove Image

Background Repeat
- No Repeat
- ◉ Tile
- Tile Horizontally
- Tile Vertically

Background Position
- ◉ Left
- Center
- Right

Background Attachment
- ◉ Fixed
- Scroll

Background repeat allows you to repeat the image over the entire background by tiling over the whole background (along both the x and y axis), tiling horizontally (only a single layer of the image on the x axis) or tiling vertically (single layer of the image along the y axis).

The next option down is to position the background in a certain place – left, centre or right. This will determine where the image is positioned before any tiling takes place. For example, if you choose right, and have chosen to tile vertically in the repeat options, then the image will be repeated in a single column down the right side of your webpage.

The final options are to either have the background image fixed, which means it stays where it is when you scroll through the content, or scroll, which means the background image scrolls (moves), with the content.

NOTE: If you choose to have the image fixed, it may not display as fixed in the actual preview pane. Therefore, save the changes and then go to your homepage URL. Here you will be able to see the fixed image effect.

I don't recommend using a background image at all. Simply colour is better as images often look messy and unprofessional. However, I do recommend you upload an image and play around with the settings to see what they do. When you have finished, click the remove image to get rid of it.

The next option is the Navigation options, which allow you to select menus to use on your site. Menus are built in another area of the dashboard, and you have total control over the contents of these menus. We will look at this later.

Next up is the Widgets menu. Clicking that will open up a screen showing you the widgetized areas of your site's template.

The Twenty Eleven theme has three footer areas, and you can click on each of these and add/remove widgets directly from this screen. We will look at adding widgets later, so let's move on.

The final options in the customize screen are for a Static Front Page.

Static Front Page

Front page displays

- ○ Your latest posts
- ⦿ A static page

Front page

— Select — ▼

Posts page

— Select — ▼

These options are identical to the ones we saw earlier in the Reading Settings.

We will look at this later.

NOTE: If you haven't created a WordPress PAGE, then you won't be able to set your front page (home page), to show a page instead of posts.

OK, when you have finished playing with the customize settings, either save and publish your changes or cancel to undo your experimentation.

Let's now go back and see how we can install new themes to completely change the look of our website.

Finding Wordpress Themes, Installing and Selecting them

We installed the Twenty Eleven theme earlier, so we know how to search for, and install a new theme.

Click on the **Themes** link under the **Appearance** menu if it is not already selected.

Click on the **Add** New button at the top of the themes screen.

Add Themes Upload Theme

15 Featured Popular Latest ⚙ Feature Filter

Search themes...

At the very top of this screen is a button, labelled "Upload Theme". If you bought, or downloaded a free theme from a website, it will come as a zip file. You can install it by clicking this button, selecting the file, and clicking Install.

There is a search box on this screen, in case you know the name of the theme you want (we used this to search for Twenty Eleven earlier).

There is also a menu at the top, with "Featured" selected by default. This will show you a list of featured themes, allowing you to choose any of those to install.

Click on the "Popular" link to be offered a list of popular Wordpress themes. This is often a good place to start, since these are the themes that have been downloaded the most, or rated the highest.

If you want to see the latest Wordpress themes to be accepted into the theme repository, click the "Latest" link.

Finally, the "Feature Filter" gives you the chance to specify exactly what you are looking for.

Add Themes   Upload Theme

| 100   Featured   Popular   Latest | ⚙ Feature Filter |

Apply Filters

Colors	Layout	Features	Subject
☐ Black	☐ Fixed Layout	☐ Accessibility Ready	☐ Holiday
☐ Blue	☐ Fluid Layout	☐ Blavatar	☐ Photoblogging
☐ Brown	☐ Responsive Layou	☐ BuddyPress	☐ Seasonal
☐ Gray	☐ One Column	☐ Custom Background	
☐ Green	☐ Two Columns	☐ Custom Colors	
☐ Orange	☐ Three Columns	☐ Custom Header	
☐ Pink	☐ Four Columns	☐ Custom Menu	
☐ Purple	☐ Left Sidebar	☐ Editor Style	
☐ Red	☐ Right Sidebar	☐ Featured Image Header	
☐ Silver		☐ Featured Images	
☐ Tan		☐ Flexible Header	
☐ White		☐ Front Page Posting	

If you want a blue, two-column theme with fixed layout, you can select these options and hit the "Apply Filters" button.

WordPress will go away and find the themes that match the features you have selected.

When you do a search (with the exception of the Upload feature which requires you to navigate to the zip file on your computer), you are presented with previews of the themes relevant to your search:

Mouse over each thumbnail image and you get the Install, Preview and Details & Preview options we saw earlier.

The preview link is well worth clicking before installing any new theme. A window opens to show you a preview of the theme, with headers, fonts, bullets etc., so you know exactly what the various aspects of your pages can look like.

If you like a particular theme, you can simply install it. If not, move onto the next one. Feel free to install a few themes. If you don't like them you can always uninstall them easily enough.

When you install a theme, you'll get presented with a menu asking what you want to do:

Installing Theme: PageLines 1.2.9

Downloading install package from `http://wordpress.org/extend/t`

Unpacking the package...

Installing the theme...

Successfully installed the theme **PageLines 1.2.9**.

Live Preview | Activate | Return to Theme Installer

I recommend you click Live Preview first to see what the theme looks like using the existing content on your site. This will show you exactly how YOUR site will look with this theme. However, you will need content on your site in order to get a good idea of how things will look.

NOTE: For some themes, the live preview will not work and you'll be forced to activate it to see how it appears and functions. If you find a theme like this, don't worry. It's easy to switch back to a previous one if you don't fancy the new design.

To switch between installed themes, go to the **Themes** page inside the **Appearance** menu. You will see the familiar current theme in the first position, and all of the other installed themes appear after as thumbnails.

If you move your mouse over the thumbnails of installed, inactive themes, you'll see the thumbnail change to include a menu:

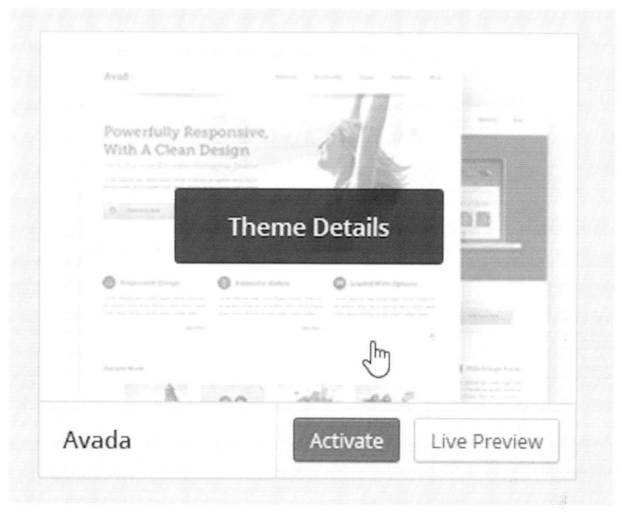

You have those familiar options.

Live Preview allows you to see what the theme will look like on your site. The Live Preview opens in the same theme customize screen we saw earlier. If you want to activate one of the installed themes, simply click the **Activate** button.

The other option you have on this thumbnail is **Theme Details**. Clicking this will bring up more details on the theme and a **Delete** link in case you want to delete a theme. How much more detail? Well that depends on the author of the theme, and how much detail they included with the theme.

NOTE: As a matter of security, I don't recommend you keep themes that you do not use. Once you have decided which theme you want to use for your site, delete all other themes using the delete link on the "Theme Details" screen.

We are going to continue working with the Twenty Eleven theme in this book, so I'll activate it and delete the other themes that are installed.

Adding a custom graphic header to your site

OK, click on the **Header** link in the **Appearance** menu.

There is a setting here that we need to explore. Essentially it allows you to upload your own graphic for the header of your website. I always create a header image for my sites that includes the Site Title and tagline.

The only thing you need to get right is to use the correct width & height for the header image. The dimensions differ depending on the theme. This screen will tell you what dimensions you need for your chosen theme.

Select Image

You can select an image to be shown at the top of your site by uploading from your computer or choosing from your media library. After selecting an image you will be able to crop it.

Images should be at least **1000 pixels** wide. Suggested width is **1000 pixels**. Suggested height is **288 pixels**.

Choose an image from your computer:

Choose File No file chosen   Upload

For the Twenty Eleven theme, the image needs to be 1000 pixels wide and 288 pixels high. Any image that is not the correct size will look distorted on the site, so do stick to the suggested image dimensions.

I have created a quick header image with just my Site Title and tagline. Let's add it to the site.

Click the **Choose File** button and select the header image from your computer. Then click the upload button to upload it to your website.

You'll then be taken to a screen showing your header and asking if you want to crop it:

 Crop Header Image

Choose the part of the image you want to use as your header

Crop and Publish | Skip Cropping, Publish Image as Is ⬅

Since my image is exactly 1000 x 288 pixels, I don't need to crop it. I can simply click the **Skip Cropping, Publish Image as Is** button.

If I now look at my homepage, there is a problem:

You can see that the site Title & Tagline are still showing.

We can remove this on the header setting screen. Scroll to the bottom and you'll see the checkbox:

Header Text

Header Text

☐ Show header text with your image.

Reset Text Color

This will restore the original header text. Y

(Restore Original Header Text)

Save Changes

Uncheck the box and then click the Save Changes button.

After reloading my homepage I can now see that everything looks fine:

Visual Wordpress

Learning Wordpress The Visual Way

Home | Search

Hello world!

Posted on October 15, 2012

Welcome to WordPress. This is your first post. Edit or delete it, then start blogging! ☺

Greatest freak out ever (ORIGINAL VIDEO) | Share | More info

META
- Site Admin
- Log out
- Entries RSS
- Comments RSS
- WordPress.org

CALENDAR

OCTOBER 2012

If you are not particularly good with graphics software, you can hire someone to create a logo for you on Fiverr.com. It'll only cost you $5! However, there is also a free software tool you can use to create a header that looks OK (and usually better than those you can get on Fiverr.com). It's called XHeader and you can watch a short video I created on using the software here:

The theme Editor menu

The bottom item in the Appearance menu is the Editor. This allows you to edit the theme template files. We won't be covering this in the book, as it is an advanced topic requiring programming skills.

OK, the last two options in the appearance menu are very important – Widgets and Menus. However, they'll actually make a lot more sense once we have some content on the site, so let's leave those until a little later on in the book.

Tasks to complete

1. Choose a theme you want to use. For your first site I recommend you stick with Twenty Eleven (you can always change it later), as we'll use it throughout this book as our reference theme.
2. Modify your theme.
3. Add a header graphic if you want a unique one.

Plugins

In this section, I want to explain what plugins are, where you can get them, and how to install them, etc. I'll also walk you through the installation and configuration of a few plugins as we go through this section. We will install more plugins later when there is something specific that we need on our site, but for now, let's concentrate on those that I feel are essential to all WordPress sites.

NOTE: from time to time, plugins get updated. Sometimes this is for feature enhancements, and other times it's so that the plugin remains compatible with an updated version of WordPress. Either or, there may be times where you could see different interfaces and perhaps some options removed (or added), from those illustrated in this book. Most modifications though, should be easy enough to figure out.

In the Dashboard Navigation bar, you'll see the Plugins menu:

The menu has three options:

Installed Plugins – To view the current list of installed plugins.

Add New – For when you want to add a new plugin.

Editor – This is a text editor that allows you to modify the code of the plugins. We won't be looking at this advanced aspect.

Click on the installed plugins menu.

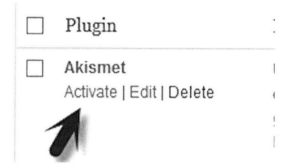

At the very top left of this screenshot you'll see where it says:

All(4) | Active (3) | Inactive (1) | Recently Active (1)

This refers to the plugins you have installed. The numbers in brackets next to each of these items tells you how many plugins are in that group. Therefore we have a total of 4 plugins installed on this site, and 1 is inactive.

To activate a plugin is easy. Just click the Activate link underneath the name of the plugin.

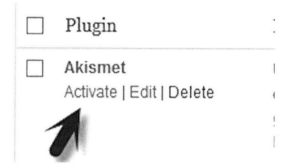

NOTE: You may also have a menu item at the top labelled Drop-ins. These are special types of plugins that alter core Wordpress functionality.

The menu at the top will change to reflect the new activated plugin. At the moment, the **All** menu item is selected.

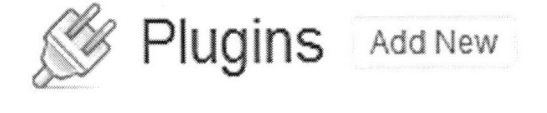 Plugins Add New

All (7) | Active (6) | Inactive (1) | Drop-ins (1)

Bulk ...ons [v] Apply

This is the filter that is currently set to show ALL plugins (active, inactive, etc).

We can view just the active, or just the inactive, by clicking those menu items.

NOTE: It is not a good idea to keep plugins installed that are inactive. If you do not need a plugin, uninstall it.

The "Drop-ins" menu may appear as you install more plugins. Drop-in plugins are special plugins that change the core functionality of Wordpress. This might be something like a caching plugin.

There may be times when another item appears in this menu labelled **Updates Available**. This will appear when there is an update available for one of your plugins and you can click this link to see which plugins have updates pending. However, I recommend you handle all updates as we saw earlier – by using the Dashboard -> Updates menu whenever you get notified there is something that needs updating.

We don't want to use either of the pre-installed plugins, so we can delete them now.

NOTE: Akismet is actually a good anti-spam plugin but it went commercial a while back, meaning it's no longer free if you have a commercial website.

Deleting plugins

To delete a plugin, it needs to be inactive. Therefore we need to deactivate the one we activated a few minutes ago before proceeding.

☐ **Hello Dolly**
Deactivate | Edit

Just click the **Deactivate** link under the plugin.

To delete a plugin, just click the Delete link under the plugin name (the delete link only appears on inactive plugins):

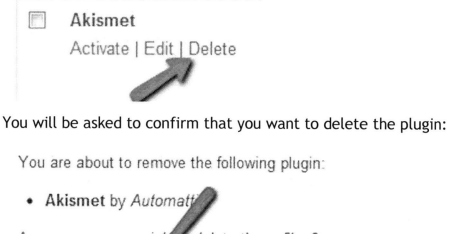

You will be asked to confirm that you want to delete the plugin:

You are about to remove the following plugin:

- **Akismet** by *Automatt*

Are you sure you wish to delete these files?

(Yes, Delete these files)   (No, Return me to the plugin list)

Click to view entire list of files which will be deleted

Clicking that button will delete the plugin and all its files from your server.

If you have more than one plugin to delete, there is a quicker way to remove multiple plugins in one go:

☐	Plugin	Description
☑	**Akismet** Activate | Edit | Delete	Used by millions, Akis **from comment and tr** sleep. To get started: Akismet API key, and Version 2.5.6 | By Auto
☑	**Hello Dolly** Activate | Edit | Delete	This is not just a plugir summed up in two wor activated you will rando on every page. Version 1.6 | By Matt I
☐	Plugin	Description

Bulk Actions ▼ (Apply)

Bulk Actions
Activate
Deactivate
Update
Delete

Just check the box next to each plugin you want to delete, then, in the **Bulk Actions** drop down box at the bottom, select **Delete**. Now click the Apply button to carry out the deletion. You will get a similar screen to the confirmation screen we saw a moment ago asking to confirm you want to delete all of the selected plugins.

NOTE: The bulk action feature also allows you to carry out other features on multiple plugins at once. These are Activate, Deactivate and Update.

Installing important plugins

Before we look at the plugins, I need to let you know that plugins are updated frequently, and their appearance may change a little. However, these changes are usually minor cosmetic changes, so if you don't see exactly what I am showing you in these screenshots, look around. The options will be there somewhere.

OK, we now have no plugins installed. So let's go ahead and install 4 very important plugins, then configure them.

WP-DBManager

This plugin is VERY important because it will look after your WordPress database (that is where all of the information needed to create your website is stored). This plugin will not only keep the database healthy by optimizing it periodically, it will also make backups of the database at pre-arranged intervals, and send you a copy of the database via email. If you ever have to "reinstall" your site, these database backups are vital.

To install any plugin, go to the **Add New** Plugin screen by clicking the button at the top of the screen, or the link in the menu:

On the Add New screen, there is a search box. Type in **wp dbmanager** and hit the rerun key on your keyboard.

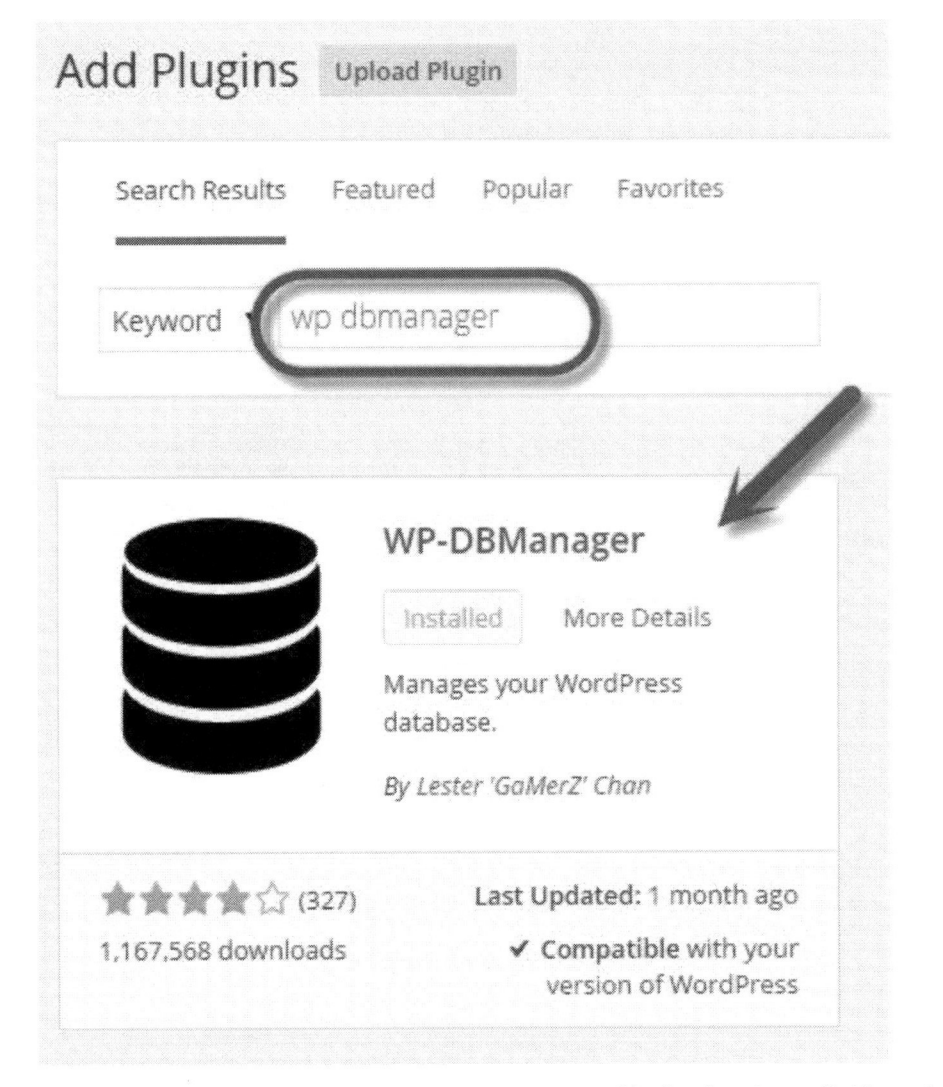

The WP-DBManager plugin will appear. Click the Install Now button (mine actually says "Installed" as I've already installed these plugins).

You'll be asked to confirm that you want to go ahead and install it.

After installation, you'll be asked what you want to do next:

Installing Plugin: WP-DE

Downloading install package from `http://downloads.`

Unpacking the package...

Installing the plugin...

Successfully installed the plugin **WP-DBManager 2.6.**

Activate Plugin | Return to Plugin Installer

Click the link to activate the plugin.

Whenever you activate a new plugin, you'll usually get a new menu item in the Dashboard Navigation menu. This new menu item can sometimes appear inside the existing **Settings** menu, or it can appear as a new top-level menu item. With this plugin, we get the latter:

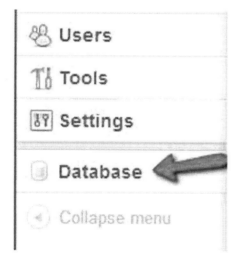

There is now a menu called "Database" in your Dashboard Navigation area.

Before we look at that in detail, there is one other thing you may have noticed. At the top of your screen there may be a warning that looks like this:

Plugins Add New

> **Your backup folder MIGHT be visible to the public**
>
> To correct this issue, move the .htaccess file from wp-content/plugins/wp-dbmanager to ▓▓▓▓▓▓▓public_html/wp-content/backup-db

This is just a warning. While you can ignore it, it is always better to fix these problems. This plugin wants to protect the folder where backups will be saved. This is to prevent unauthorized people from downloading your database copies. To do this, we need to move & rename a file that was installed with the plugin. If you know how to use FTP, then you can use that. However, since I suspect many of you may not know how to use FTP, I'll show you how to do this in your cPanel.

Login to the cPanel of your hosting account.

Scroll down to the section on files, and click on the File Manager link.

You will be asked where you want to login to:

File Manager Directory Selection

Please select a directory to open:

- ○ Home Directory
- ○ Web Root (public_html/www)
- ○ Public FTP Root (public_ftp)
- ⦿ Document Root for:

☑ Show Hidden Files (dotfiles).

☐ Skip this question, and always open this directory in the future when opening File Manager.

Go

Select the bottom option of **Document Root for:** and select your domain name in the drop down box. Click the Go button to access your web space for the site. It will open in a new tab in your browser.

The file manager is very similar to the type of File Manager you have used with Microsoft Windows or on your Mac computer.

On the right hand side of the File Manager you will see the files & folders inside your currently selected folder (which is the document root we selected a moment ago). The left side you can see other folders on your server, but we can ignore those for now.

Glance down the column to the right of the folder list until you find **wp-content**. Double click the folder icon to the left of the folder name to open it.

	Name	Size	Last Modified (GMT Dayli	Type
📁	wp-admin	4 KB	Oct 16, 2012 1:00 PM	httpd/unix-directory
📁	wp-content	4 KB	Today 9:49 AM	httpd/unix-directory
📁	wp-includes	4 KB	Oct 16, 2012 1:00 PM	httpd/unix-directory
📄	.ftpquota	14 bytes	Oct 16, 2012 8:08 AM	text/x-generic
📄	.htaccess	236 bytes	Oct 17, 2012 12:12 PM	text/x-generic

OK, you are now in the wp-content folder. Now look for the **Plugins** folder and double click the folder icon next to that:

	Name	Size	Last Modified (GMT Dayli	Type
📁	backup-db	4 KB	Today 9:49 AM	httpd/t
📁	plugins	4 KB	Today 9:47 AM	httpd/t
📁	themes	4 KB	Oct 17, 2012 6:53 PM	httpd/t
📁	upgrade	4 KB	Today 9:47 AM	httpd/t
📁	uploads	4 KB	Oct 17, 2012 11:47 AM	httpd/t
📄	index.php	30 bytes	May 4, 2007 10:48 PM	text/x-

We are now inside the plugins folder. Any plugins that you install will usually have their own folder within this folder. We want the wp-dbmanager folder, so find that and double click its folder icon to open it.

Name	Size	Last Modified (GMT Dayli	Type
wp-dbmanager	4 KB	Today 9:47 AM	httpd/u
index.php	30 bytes	Apr 15, 2009 8:57 PM	text/x-

OK, great. You should now see a list of files. Find the one called **htaccess.txt** and right click on it to open a popup menu.

Select **Move** from this menu.

OK, now we need to go back and check the error message that we received in the Dashboard. Here is mine. I want to copy down the last part of the destination URL:

In my case, it's **wp-content/backup-db**. The chances are that yours will be the same.

Now in the File Manager, edit the line in the lower box so that after the **/wp-content/** part of the URL, it just says **backup-db** (as shown in the error message above).

Here is mine:

Click the Move File(s) button to move the htaccess.txt file.

OK, now we need to locate that file and rename it.

At the top of the File Manager, there is a button to move **Up One Level**.

Click it.

Click it a second time and you should now see the backup-db folder:

Double click the folder icon to the left of the folder name to open it.

You should now see the htaccess.txt file that we moved here:

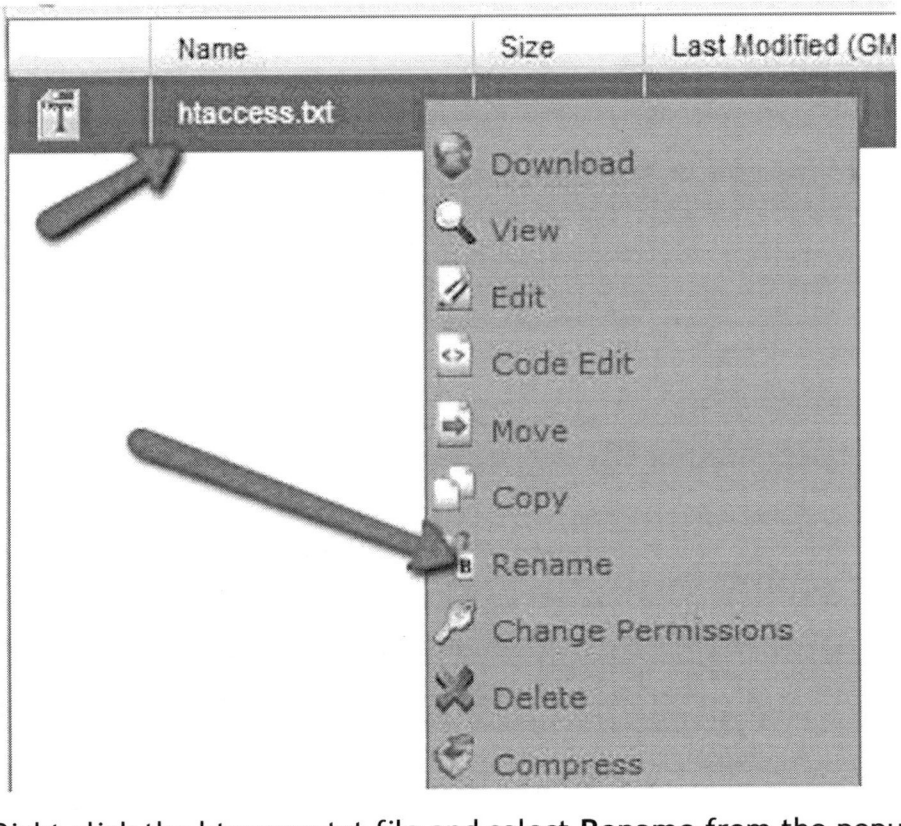

Right click the htaccess.txt file and select **Rename** from the popup menu.

In the screen that appears, edit the lower box that contains the file name. Remove the **.txt** from the end of the filename and ADD a period (full stop) to the beginning of the filename. The filename should end up as **.htaccess**

Click the rename file button to complete the process.

You can now close the File Manager and logout of your cPanel.

Go back to your WordPress Dashboard where the error message is displayed and click the Refresh button on your web browser's toolbar. The error message should disappear.

Great. Let's configure the WP-DBManager plugin so we can start getting backups of our database emailed to us.

From the **Database** Menu, select **DB Options.**

Just scroll to the bottom of that page and click the **Save Changes** button (I know you didn't make any changes, but click the button anyway). By doing this, you'll activate the plugin.

Automatic Scheduling

Automatic Backing Up Of DB: Next backup date: June 28, 2013 @ 8:57 am

Every `1`   Week(s) `v`   Gzip `No` `v`

E-mail backup to: `juicinglife@gmail.com`   (Leave blank to disable this

WP-DBManager can automatically backup your database after a certain period.

Automatic Optimizing Of DB: Next optimize date: **June 28, 2013 @ 8:57 am**

Every `3`   Day(s) `v`

WP-DBManager can automatically optimize your database after a certain period.

Automatic Repairing Of DB: Next repair date: **June 28, 2013 @ 8:57 am**

Every `2`   Week(s) `v`

WP-DBManager can automatically repair your database after a certain period.

Now, under the automatic scheduling section you should see today's date and (serve) time. That means the first backup was created and emailed to you. It was sent to the same address found in the **Backup Email Options** "To" box on this page. That email will be the same one we filled in earlier, but if you want to change it to a different email, you can.

You'll see that automatic optimizing of the database will occur every 3 days, and automatic repair of the database every 2 weeks.

These are the default settings. If you add content to your site daily, you might like to get the backup sent more frequently than the once a week default (top box in the screenshot above), so you could change that to every 3 or 4 days, or whatever suites your needs.

The only other thing you may want to change is the GZip setting at the top. The default is no, meaning the backup is not compressed. Compressing makes the backup considerably smaller, so I do recommend you change this to Yes, and save changes.

Other than that, you are all set up with this plugin.

Go check your email to see if the first backup has arrived.

Contact Form 7

The Contact Form is another important part of a website because it allows people to contact you privately. The plugin we are going to install is called **Contact Form 7**, so go to the **Add New** plugin page and search for that exact phrase.

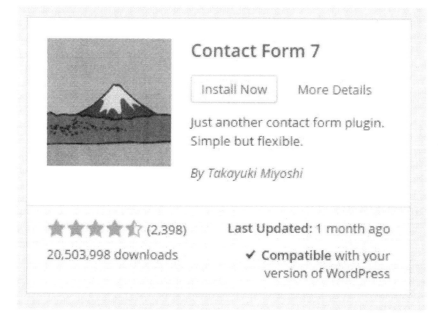

When you find it (it should be the first item in the list), click the Install Now link under the plugin name.

When prompted, activate the plugin. This one will create a menu in the Dashboard Navigation called **Contact**.

When you click on the menu item, you'll be taken to the contact form screen that shows all active contact forms (you can use this plugin to create different forms for different purposes).

	Title	Shortcode
☐	Contact form 1	[contact-form-7 id="50" title="Contact form 1"]
☐	Title	Shortcode

There is one form in the list – the default one that the plugin set up. You can go in and edit this form by clicking the name of the form (Contact form 1), on the left. The title is a hyperlink to the form's editor screen.

We'll use the form as it is because it is fully functional and contains the important information.

What we need to do is copy the **shortcode** listed on the right.

[contact-form-7 id="50" title="Contact form 1"]

A shortcode is a convenient code for inserting something into a webpage. Some plugins use them, some don't. They make adding features to pages very simple.

Copy the code, and then go over to the **Add New** PAGE (NOT post) screen:

You'll have a new, blank page.

Add the word **Contact** in the title box, and paste the shortcode into the body of the page as shown below:

Contact

Permalink: http://com-vip.org/contact/ (Edit) (View Page)

Upload/Insert 🖼️   Visual | HTML

| B | *I* | ABC | ☰ | ☰ | 66 | ☰ | ☰ | ☰ | 🔗 | 🔗 | ⬚ | ABC▼ | ⬚ | ⬚ |

| Paragraph ▼ | U | ▬ | A ▼ | 📋 | 📋 | ⬚ | Ω | ⬚ | ⬚ | ↺ | ↻ | ❓ |

[contact-form-7 id="50" title="Contact form 1"]

Click the Publish button on the right to publish this page to your site.

If you now visit your site, you will see that WordPress has automatically added a new menu item at the top, called **Contact** (the title of the page we just created).

Clicking it takes you to your new contact page on the site:

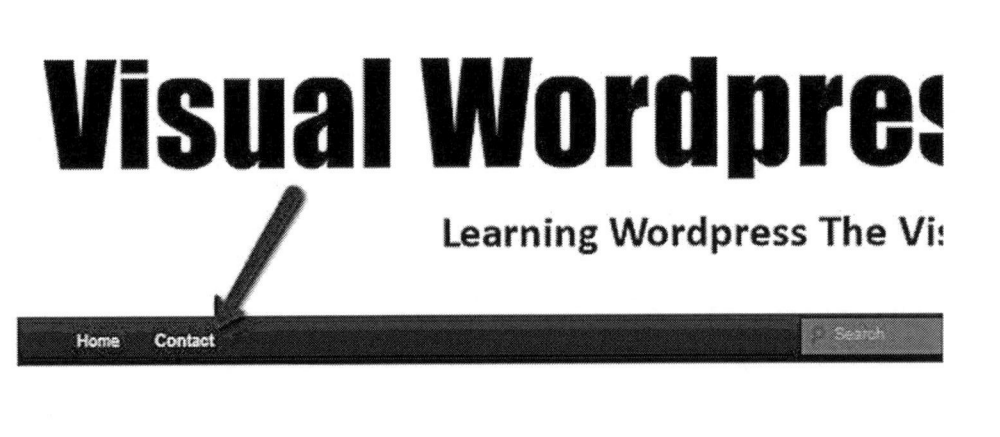

Contact

Your Name (required)

Your Email (required)

Subject

Your Message

Send

Great, now visitors can contact us.

Auto Terms of Service and Privacy Policy

This plugin adds a few other essential pages to the website, like the privacy policy and terms of service.

Go to the Add New plugin and search for **auto terms**.

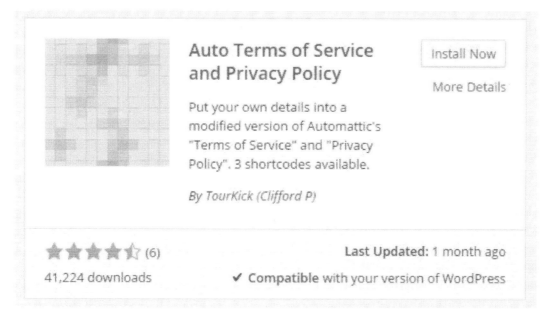

Auto Terms of Service and Privacy Policy

Install Now

More Details

Put your own details into a modified version of Automattic's "Terms of Service" and "Privacy Policy". 3 shortcodes available.

By TourKick (Clifford P)

★★★★⯪ (6)

41,224 downloads

Last Updated: 1 month ago

✔ **Compatible** with your version of WordPress

Install and activate the plugin.

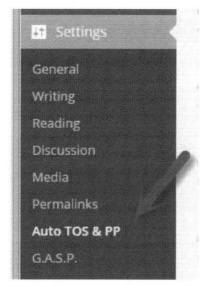

Click on the **Settings** menu followed by the **Auto TOS & PP**.

There is a form on this screen that you need to fill. It's fairly intuitive, so go ahead and fill it in.

Make sure that you have the top option set to show your policies:

On/Off:

Enter all your info below, then Turn On so shortcodes can work. Will not allow you to Turn On until you enter all required (*) fields.

On / Displaying ▼

Once done, click on the Save button at the bottom.

Now, we need to create some pages, but before we leave this screen, copy and paste the "shortcodes" at the top, into a text editor so you have easy access to them in as we create the pages.

Available shortcodes:

[my_terms_of_service_and_privacy_policy]

[my_terms_of_service]

[my_privacy_policy]

Now, under the **Pages** menu in the sidebar, click **Add New.**

Enter the title "Privacy Policy", and in the large rectangular editor window, paste in the shortcode for the privacy policy:

Add New Page

Privacy Policy

Permalink: http://rapidwpsites.com/privacy-policy/ [Edit] [View Page]

[Add Media] [Add Form]

| B | *I* | ABC | | | " | — | | | | | | | | | |

Paragraph ▼ U ≡ A ▼ 🖍 ⊘ Ω ⇥ ⇤ ↰ ↱ ❓

[my_privacy_policy]

Now click the **Publish** button on the right.

Once the page is published, click the View Page button to see your new Privacy Policy.

Repeat this process, adding a page for the Terms of Service (call the page title simply "Terms").

OK; with that completed, you now have a Privacy Policy and Terms of Service page created.

WordPress SEO

Go to the **Add New** plugin page and search for **WordPress SEO**.

This is the one you want by "Yoast":

WordPress SEO by Yoast

Update Now

More Details

Improve your WordPress SEO:
Write better content and have a
fully optimized WordPress site
using Yoast's WordPress SEO
plugin.

By Team Yoast

★★★★½ (3,517)

13,244,213 downloads

Last Updated: 14 mins ago

✔ **Compatible** with your version of WordPress

Install and activate the plugin.

This plugin installs a new menu in the Dashboard Navigation called SEO.

SEO

Dashboard

Titles & Metas

Social

XML Sitemaps

Permalinks

Internal Links

RSS

Import & Export

Bulk Editor

Edit Files

Extensions

There are a number of options in this menu, but we'll only look at the essential ones.

The first item in the menu is **Dashboard**. If you click on that you can see a few settings - we'll leave all of these with their default values.

The next item in the menu is **Titles & Metas**. Click on it.

112

There are a number of tabs across the top of "Titles & Metas" and we will look at them, but first, on the General tab, check the **Noindex subpages of archives** checkbox found in the "Sitewide meta settings" section. Click the Save Changes button at the bottom.

This setting will help prevent unnecessary duplication of content on your site.

We can ignore the "Home" tab as there is nothing to set here.

Click on to the "Post Types" tab.

You will see options for Posts, Pages, Media and Views. The options for each of these are similar:

Posts

Title template:	%%title%% %%page%% %%sep%% %%sitename%%
Meta description template:	
Meta Robots:	☐ noindex, follow
Date in Snippet Preview:	☐ Show date in snippet preview?
WordPress SEO Meta Box:	☐ Hide

In the Title template section, you can see "variables". These variables are swapped out for real information when a page is rendered in a web browser. For example, the %%title%% variable will be replaced by the title of the actual web page (which you enter when adding the post or page. %%sitename%% will be replaced with your site's name (defined in the settings).

For a full list of variables you can use, click on the Help tab at the top right, then click on the Basic or Advanced Variables tabs on the left. You'll see a list of all variables that are available to you:

113

Basic Variables

Template explanation	
Basic Variables	
Advanced Variables	

Variable	Description
%%date%%	Replaced with the date of the post/page
%%title%%	Replaced with the title of the post/page
%%parent_title%%	Replaced with the title of the parent page of the current
%%sitename%%	The site's name
%%sitedesc%%	The site's tag line / description
%%excerpt%%	Replaced with the post/page excerpt (or auto-generated
%%excerpt_only%%	Replaced with the post/page excerpt (without auto-gener
%%tag%%	Replaced with the current tag/tags
%%category%%	Replaced with the post categories (comma separated)
%%category_description%%	Replaced with the category description
%%tag_description%%	Replaced with the tag description
%%term_description%%	Replaced with the term description
%%term_title%%	Replaced with the term name

OK, so how do you take advantage of these variables, and set it up for your site?

What I recommend you do for ALL titles on your site is to use a combination of your site name and the post/page title. You can have your site name first or last (I recommend last), so that a post title on your site might look like this:

How to add a plugin to your site :: VisualWordPress.com

NOTE: The domain name I used in this example is not a real domain name - at least not mine. It is just used as an example.

Each post on our site will have a different title, so in the title template box for posts, we MUST use a variable that represents the title - %%title%%.

We also want the site name included in the title, but that won't change for each post because the site name is always the site name. We can therefore type that in manually, but to get you used to using variables, let's use one for the site name as well.

So there are two variables needed for the post titles:

%%sitename%%

%%title%%

The title template would look something like this:

%%title%% :: %%sitename%%

Then whenever a post on your site is loaded in a web browser by a visitor, %%title%% will be swapped for the title of the post or page, and %%sitename%% will be swapped for your site's name.

OK, now we have that template, copy it into all of the title template boxes on this Post Type screen. There should be 4 - posts, pages, media & views.

The next choice we have is what we want displayed for the Meta description. On posts, I recommend you use the excerpt of the post. The variable for excerpts is:

%%excerpt%%

Paste that into the Meta description box of the Posts section.

NOTE: We'll cover excerpts later when we look into writing posts, but basically when we add a new post to our site, we add in a short description of that post in an excerpt box. That will then be used as the post description when the page loads.

For the Pages, Media and Views sections, leave the Meta description boxes empty. They are not important pages on the site (see the discussion earlier of pages v posts), so they don't need a Meta description tag.

Underneath the posts, pages and media sections you'll see some check boxes.

Title template:	%%title%% :: %%sitename%%
Meta description template:	
Meta Robots:	☐ noindex, follow
Date in Snippet Preview:	☐ Show date in snippet preview?
WordPress SEO Meta Box:	☐ Hide

The top item is related to the Meta Robots. These tell search engines how to deal with that type of content on your site.

If you check the box next to **noindex, follow**, then Google will not index that type of content, but it will follow links on those pages. For our posts, this is obviously not what we want, so leave it unchecked.

The other two options can be ignored, so leave all three boxes unchecked for each of the post types. I usually check the **noindex, follow** for Pages only, since the way I use pages (and the way I teach you to use pages in this book) means I don't really want them indexed in Google.

NOTE: The settings you see for posts, pages and media are global settings. All of these can be over-ridden at the individual post or page level, so we'll leave all of these unchecked.

OK, to summarize the changes we have made to Post types, we have set ALL title templates to:

%%title%% :: %%sitename%%

The post description was set to:

%%excerpt%%

All other settings are left blank.

Scroll to the bottom and click the Save Changes button.

Now click on the **Taxonomies** tab. The important settings on this screen are for the category and tag pages.

We haven't looked at categories or tags yet, so this may be a little confusing. For now, just enter the values I tell you and we'll see how these affect our site later when we have some content up there.

Categories:

Categories

Title template:	%%category%% on %%sitename%%
Meta description template:	%%category_description%%
Meta Robots:	☑ noindex, follow
WordPress SEO Meta Box:	☐ Hide

%%Category%% inserts the category name into the title. The description is the category description that we'll look at later when discussing categories.

I recommend that you select the **noindex, follow checkbox** for categories so that Google will read the pages and follow the links to the posts on your site, but NOT index the category page as this can contain a lot of duplicate content on the site.

NOTE: For experienced users, I actually recommend category pages be indexed (by un-checking this box), but you do need to make changes to your WordPress template and the way you use the category pages to prevent unnecessary content duplication. For this book, we'll stick with the easier option of checking the box.

Tags:

Tags

Title template:	Posts related to %%tag%% on %%sitename%%
Meta description template:	%%tag_description%%
Meta Robots:	☑ noindex, follow
WordPress SEO Meta Box:	☐ Hide

%%tag%% is replaced by the tag, and %%tag_description%% is replaced by the description we gave to that tag (we'll see this later when discussing tags).

Just like the category pages, I recommend you check the **noindex, follow** checkbox. This will prevent the search engines from indexing the tag pages, but allow them to spider the page, follow the links and find all of the posts on your site.

NOTE: Again, as with categories, I actually recommend advanced users allow the tag pages to be indexed, but you do need to customize your template/theme so that the tag pages don't end up with lots of duplicate content. This type of work is beyond the scope of this book.

Format:

Format	
Title template:	%%term_title%% Archives %%page%% %%sep%% %%sitename%%
Meta description template:	
Meta Robots:	☑ noindex, follow
WordPress SEO Meta Box:	☐ Hide

This one is just left at the default settings. If your settings are a little different to those above, just leave your settings as they are.

OK, the final tab is the **Other** tab. Click on it now.

This tab contains settings for some "archive" pages.

Here are the settings for **Author Pages:**

Author Archives

Title template:

%%name%%, Author at %%sitename%%

Meta description template:

Meta Robots:
☑ noindex, follow

☐ Disable the author archives

If you're running a one author blog, the author archive will always look exactly the same as your homepage. And even though you may not link to it, others might, to do you harm. Disabling them here will make sure any link to those archives will be 301 redirected to the homepage.

Make sure the Meta robots option is checked to **noindex, follow**. This again is to prevent unnecessary duplication of content on the site.

For **Date Archives:**

Date Archives

Title template:

%%date%% %%sep%% %%sitename%%

Meta description template:

Meta Robots:
☑ noindex, follow

☐ Disable the date-based archives

For the date based archives, the same applies: they probably look a lot like your homepage, and could thus be seen as duplicate content.

Again, **noindex, follow**.

And for the **special pages:**

Special Pages

These pages will be noindex, followed by default, so they will never show up in search results.

Search pages

Title template:

You searched for %%searchphrase%% %%sep%% %%sitename%%

404 pages

Title template:

Page Not Found %%sep%% %%sitename%%

Save Settings

These format the titles for the search results (when using the built in search feature of WordPress), page and the 404 page is used when a page is not found.

Save settings when complete.

OK, we are finished with the WordPress SEO plugin settings for the moment, although we will see them again later in another part of the Dashboard.

There is a huge amount of functionality built into this WordPress SEO plugin. We won't be covering all the settings in this book. The only other option I want to cover here is the XML Sitemaps. Click on that option in the menu.

XML Sitemap

☑ Check this box to enable XML sitemap functionality.

You can find your XML Sitemap here: [XML Sitemap]

You do **not** need to generate the XML sitemap, nor will it take up time to generate after publishing a post.

User sitemap

☑ Disable author/user sitemap

General settings

After content publication, the plugin automatically pings Google and Bing, do you need it to ping other search engines too? If so, check the box:

☑ Ping Yahoo!
☑ Ping Ask.com

The top checkbox is to enable the Sitemap feature of WordPress SEO. If you decide to use a different plugin for sitemaps, make sure this one is unchecked. However, the sitemap features of this plugin integrate totally with the rest of the SEO settings on the site, so I recommend you use this one and check the box.

I'd also recommend you check the Ping Yahoo and Ping Ask.com boxes. This will let those sites know when new content is added to your site. We also have a long ping list that we set up earlier in the book when dealing with writing settings, so a lot of places will be informed when new content is added.

Exclude post types

Please check the appropriate box below if there's a post type that you do **NOT** want to include in your sitemap:

- [ ] Posts (`post`)
- [x] Pages (`page`)
- [x] Media (`attachment`)

Exclude taxonomies

Please check the appropriate box below if there's a taxonomy that you do **NOT** want to include in your sitemap:

- [ ] Categories (`category`)
- [ ] Tags (`post_tag`)
- [x] Format (`post_format`)

Entries per page

Please enter the maximum number of entries per sitemap page (defaults to 1000, you might want to lower this to prevent memory issues on some installs):

Max entries per sitemap page: [   ]

Save Changes

In the exclude post types, I'd recommend selecting media and pages. Any media we use will be embedded into a post and doesn't need a direct link in the sitemap. Also, since pages are only being used for our "legal" content, we don't need them on the sitemap. The only links we really want showing on the sitemap are our important posts.

Finally, you have the option to exclude Category pages, Tag pages or Format from the sitemap. I recommend you leave the first two unchecked so that they are included in the sitemap. You can check the Format (post_format) option. We have set up the SEO plugin to not index the category and tag pages, but we still want the search engines to find them and follow all links on those pages.

When you're done, click the **Save Settings** button at the bottom, and your sitemap will be set up.

You can now view your sitemap by clicking the **XML Sitemap** button at the top of the

XML Sitemap settings page. The sitemap will open in a new.

XML Sitemap

Generated by Yoast's **WordPress SEO plugin**, this is an XML Sitemap, meant for const

You can find more information about XML sitemaps on **sitemaps.org**.

This XML Sitemap Index file contains 4 sitemaps.

Sitemap	Last Modified
http://rapidwpsites.com/post-sitemap.xml	2014-09-09 10:33
http://rapidwpsites.com/category-sitemap.xml	2014-09-09 10:33
http://rapidwpsites.com/post_tag-sitemap.xml	2014-09-09 10:33
http://rapidwpsites.com/frm_tag-sitemap.xml	2014-10-08 10:00

Assuming you have a post on your site, you will see at least two sitemaps, maybe more. There will be a sitemap dedicated to the posts on your site, one for the category pages, another for tag pages, and so on.

Another sitemap plugin I have used in the past did not separate out the sitemap entries like this, but lumped them all into one. I actually prefer that they be separated which is why I moved to using the Sitemap features built into the Yoast WordPress SEO plugin.

The only other setting you might like to change in this plugin is found on the permalinks page.

Permalink Settings

☐ Strip the category base (usually `/category/`) from the category URL.
☐ Enforce a trailing slash on all category and tag URL's

The top check box allows you to have the "/category/" part of a category page URL removed.

Remember we discussed the word **category** being inserted into category page URLs (and the word **tag** into tag page URLs) and how we could change that by entering a category base in the Permalinks settings? Well this option allows you to remove the word **category** altogether from the URLs of the category pages.

So, instead of creating a URL like this for my "plugins" category page:

http://visualworpdress.com/category/plugins

By checking that **Strip the category base**....option the URL would be this instead:

http://visualWordPress.com/plugins

What do I recommend? Well actually, I recommend you leave the word category in there. It doesn't do any harm and it does help identify that page to the search engines and visitor as a category page. The choice is yours. It's easy enough to change, but change it now if you are going to, before you start working on your site. Changing this later will change the URLs on your site, confusing search engines that have already indexed your old URLs.

We'll be looking at other WordPress SEO settings on a post by post (and page by page) nature, but for now we can forget about it and turn to another important part of your website – the comment system.

Tasks to complete

1. Delete any pre-installed plugins.
2. Install WP-DBManager and set it up.
3. Install Contact Form 7 and set up a contact page.
4. Install WP-Policies and create the "legal" pages.
5. Install WordPress SEO and configure it.
6. Set up the WordPress SEO plugin to handle your sitemaps.

Comments

I mentioned earlier that a lot of people turn comments OFF because they cannot be bothered with the work involved in moderating comments. The way I see it, the comments are part of the life and soul of a website and help to keep visitors engaged with you and your content. You NEED to offer them the chance to connect with you. Therefore, you really should keep comments turned on.

We have already configured the "discussion" settings to blacklist comments with known spam content (using the blacklist you found by searching on Google), but we can add another layer of protection – a comment spam plugin.

Let's install that plugin now.

Mouse over the Plugins menu and select Add New:

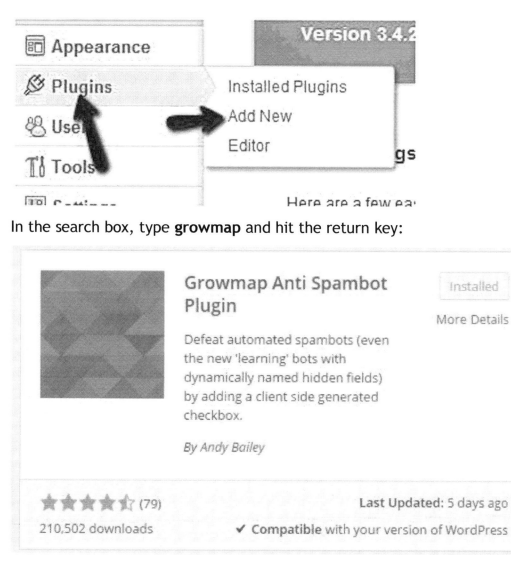

In the search box, type **growmap** and hit the return key:

The plugin we are installing is called Growmap Anti Spambot Plugin.

Click the **Install Now** link under that plugin in the search results.

Once it is installed, you'll be prompted with a choice.

 Installing Plugin: Growmap Anti Spambot I

Downloading install package from http://downloads.wordpress.org/plugin/

Unpacking the package...

Installing the plugin...

Successfully installed the plugin **Growmap Anti Spambot Plugin 1.2**.

Activate Plugin | Return to Plugin Installer

Click Activate the Plugin.

OK, that's it. The plugin has been installed.

If you mouse over the **Settings** menu you will find a new entry called G.A.S.P. These are the settings for this plugin, so click the link.

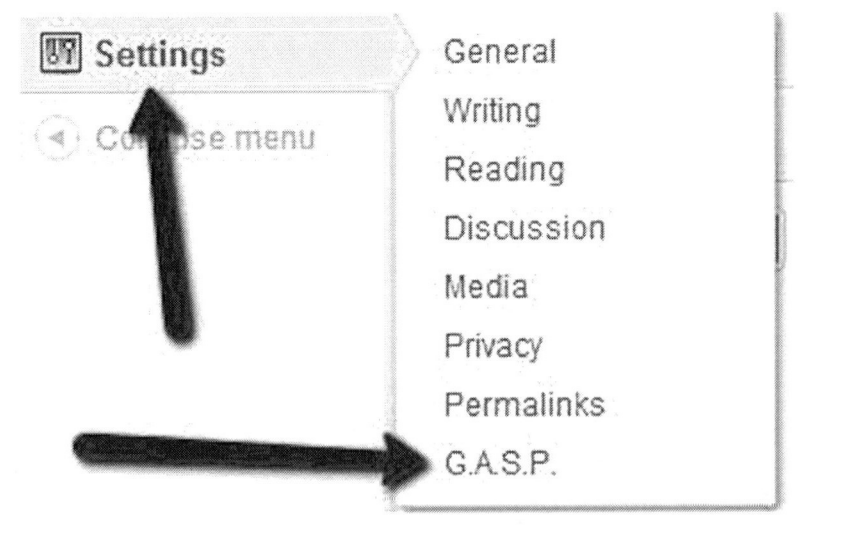

On the settings page there are quite a few options. At the very top:

Growmap Anti Spambot Plugin Settings Page

Version 1.5.5 GASP has caught this many bot comments : **0** (This does not count people who do not check the box)

Checkbox Label	Confirm you are NOT a spammer
Checkbox Name	ci_check_8a4
	You can change this if you find that bots have started to target your blog again
Secret Key updated	☑ Use secret key? 8a41d2286a463752721a64cd2a6d135d8a41d2286a463752721a64cd2a6d1
	this another bit of security to secure your comment form. You can change this to any value (letters and nu
Allow Trackbacks?	☐ Unchecking the box will prevent ALL trackbacks) See this plugin if you want a trackback validation plugin that works well with GASP Simple Trackba

Check the **Secret Key** option, and uncheck the **Allow Trackbacks.** Trackbacks are often faked and are the cause of many spam comments. I like to cut them off here.

Now scroll down to the **Heuristics** part of the page.

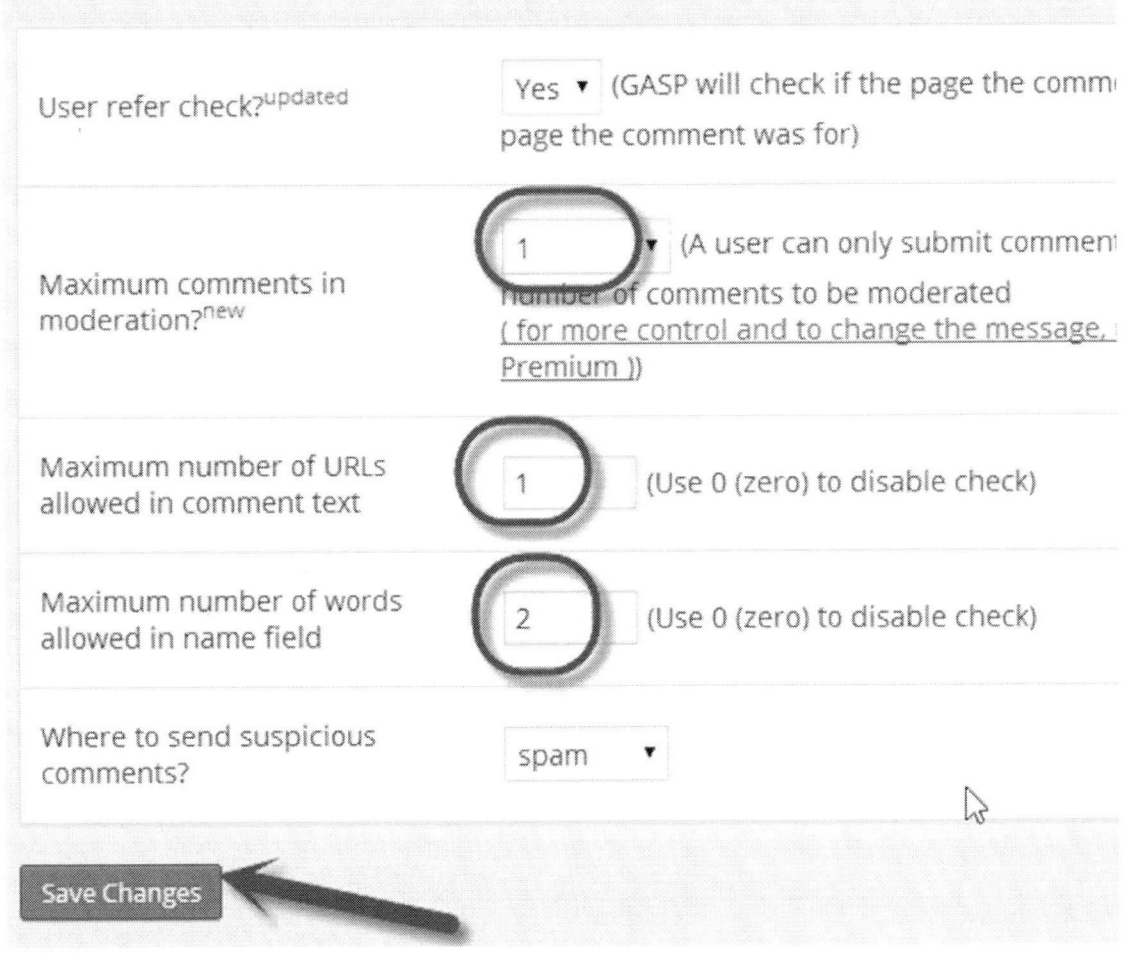

Heuristics (optional spam detection)

You can have more advanced spam detection by setting these options. Many thanks to @dragc

User refer check?[updated]	Yes ▾ (GASP will check if the page the comm page the comment was for)
Maximum comments in moderation?[new]	1 ▾ (A user can only submit commen number of comments to be moderated (for more control and to change the message, Premium))
Maximum number of URLs allowed in comment text	1 (Use 0 (zero) to disable check)
Maximum number of words allowed in name field	2 (Use 0 (zero) to disable check)
Where to send suspicious comments?	spam ▾

Save Changes

Change the **Maximum comments in moderation** to 1.

Change Maximum URLs in comment text to 1.

Optionally, change the maximum number of words in name field to 2. Some legitimate comment authors will add more than two words, but you can always check your spam folder for these that slip through. The problem with allowing multiple words in the name field is that spammers often use "money" phrases in their name field, to get a keyword rich anchor text link back to their site.

When done, click the Save Changes button.

Let's see what this plugin does (you will need to be logged out of your Dashboard to see the plugin at work).

If you look at the comment form on a post on your site, you'll see a little checkbox:

Most comment spam comes from "robot" software that won't know it has to check a box to post a comment. Anyone or anything that tries to leave a comment without checking this box will find their comment redirected to the spam folder automatically.

What if a legitimate person leaves a comment but forgets to check the box?

Well don't worry, they will get a visual warning that they forgot to check the box and have another chance to check it.

Please check the box to confirm that you are NOT a spammer

OK

This is one of the best ways to stop large amounts of spam comments.

Moderating comments

When people comment, their comments won't go live until you approve them. This is how we set the site up earlier. If you had comments set on auto-approve, you'd most likely find so many spam comments on your site that you'd be pulling your hair out. Manual approval is the only way to go, and it does not have to take a long time.

Let's see how easy it is to moderate comments.

If you click on the Comments link in the sidebar of your Dashboard, you are taken to the comments section.

Across the top is a menu with Pending, Approved, Spam, Trash:

All | Pending (1) | Approved | Spam (1) | Trash (0)

Bulk Actions ▾ Apply   Show all comment types ▾ Filter

☐	Author	Comment
☐	Andy Williams asdasd@gmailc.om 2.139.74.38	Submitted on 2012/10/18 at 12:10 This comment is OK because I used two words in my name. Approve | Reply | Quick Edit | Edit | Spam | Trash
☐	Author	Comment

Bulk Actions ▾ Apply

Lower down you can see a comment I added to my site. This comment was OK and passed all the tests – it did not have a URL in the comment, maximum two words in name, no words found in the blacklist, email address not in blacklist, etc.

If you hover your mouse over a comment in the list, a menu appears underneath that comment, which you can click to Approve, Reply, Quick Edit, Edit, send to Spam or send to Trash.

If the comment is OK, click the Approve link. If the comment is spam, click the Trash link (you don't need to use the spam link at all because we want to send all spam straight to the trash). You can also edit comments if you want to remove something or correct a spelling error - for example - from an otherwise good comment.

I recommend you don't reply to comments until you approve them. My typical workflow is this:

1. Moderate comments.
2. Go to the Approved comments by clicking the Approved link at the top.
3. Reply to comments that need a reply.
4. Go to Trash and empty it.

In the screenshot above, you will see that there is a (1) next to the spam link. That tells me there is one comment in the spam folder. It must have triggered one of the criteria we have set up for spam. Click on the spam link to see what the comment is:

	Author	Comment
☐	Author	Comment
☐	**Andy Williams Jr.** asdasd@gmail.com 2.139.74.38	Submitted on 2012/10/18 at 12:10 This comment ends up in Spam because I have three words in my name. Not Spam | Delete Permanently
☐	Author	Comment

Bulk Actions ▾ (Apply)   (Empty Spam) ⬅

Looking at the comment, you can see that my name has three words so was sent to the spam folder. If you decide that a particular comment is not spam, mouse over it and the menu appears underneath. Click the **Not Spam** link and the comment will be sent to the **Pending** pile so that you can approve it.

Note that if all comments in the spam folder are actually spam, then you can click the Empty Spam button at the bottom to delete them all at once.

When you do delete spam, it is permanently removed.

The Trash folder holds all comments that were sent to the trash. Like the Spam folder, you can retrieve comments that are in the trash (if you need to), using the mouse over menu for any comment.

Finally, we have the Approved list. These are all comments on your site that have been approved. Click the link in the menu at the top to view them.

All comments in the Approved list have a mouse over menu as well, allowing you to **Reply** to the comment if you want to. You can of course change your mind about an "approved comment", and send it to Trash if you want to, or even unapprove it if you want to think about it.

What kinds of Comments should you send to Trash?

You will get a number of comments that say things you like to hear, like "nice blog", or "Great job". I suggest you trash all comments like this because they are spam comments. Their only purpose is to try and get a backlink from your site to theirs.

I recommend you only approve comments that:

1. Add something to the main article, either with more information, opinions or constructive information. That means never approving a comment that could have been written without that person ever reading your post. Comments MUST add something to your content. If they don't I suggest you send them to the Trash.

2. Never approve a comment where the person has used a keyword phrase for their name. You'll see people using things like "best Viagra online", or "buy XYZ online" as their name. No matter how good the comment is, trash it. What many spammers do is copy a paragraph from a good webpage on another website and use that as their comment. The comment looks great, but it was copied from another website.

3. I would suggest you never approve trackbacks or pingbacks. Most will not be real anyway.

With comments, be vigilant and don't allow poor comments onto your site as they will reflect badly on both you and your website.

Here are three spammy comments left on one of my websites. All three would go straight to the trash without hesitation:

☐	Author	Comment
☐	**Del** del_minter@yahoo.com 89.143.144.226	Submitted on 2012/09/27 at 3:12 am I could not refrain from commenting. Well written! Garden Furniture
☐	**Jason** jasonphilips@gmail.com 178.73.216.89	Submitted on 2012/08/06 at 3:51 pm Very nice post. I just stumbled upon your blog and wished to say that I've truly enjoyed browsing your blog posts. In any case I will be subscribing to your feed and I hope you write again very soon!
☐	**Horizon Health and fitness EX : 58 An ellpitcal machine** annettpassmore@google mail.com 93.86.204.104	Submitted on 2012/08/06 at 2:38 pm In fact no matter if someone doesn't be aware of after that its up to other users that they will assist, so here it takes place.

None of these comments add anything to the article I wrote, meaning they made absolutely no reference to the post in question.

Did you also notice the name of the person in that last comment? That is an example of someone trying to get a keyword rich link back to their site.

Tasks to complete

1. Install Growmap and configure it.

2. Whenever there are comments on your site, moderate them. Delete any comments that are not "adding to the conversation".

Media Library

You can get to the Media Library either by clicking on the Media link in the menu, the media library sub-menu, or even when entering a piece of content:

The media library is where you can upload images, videos and other files to use on your blog. It is a convenient place to hold all your media. Uploading stuff is really very easy.

You will usually add media directly from the **Add Post** screen when typing a piece of content. However, if for example you have a lot of images that you want to upload at any one time, it is often quicker to do it directly in the Media library.

How to Upload New Media

Click on the **Add New** item in the Media menu (see screenshot above), or on the Media Library page, click the Add New button at the top.

Uploading media is as simple as dragging and dropping it onto the large, box on the screen:

(You can also click the "Select Files" button and select them directly from your hard disk.)

To drag and drop something, simply open up Windows Explorer and find the item you want to upload. Click and hold on the item and drag it over to the rectangle in the media library and drop it (unclick the mouse button).

You can see I have dragged an image of apples over the box. When I drop it there, the image is uploaded to my library. When the upload is complete, you'll be shown a thumbnail of the image:

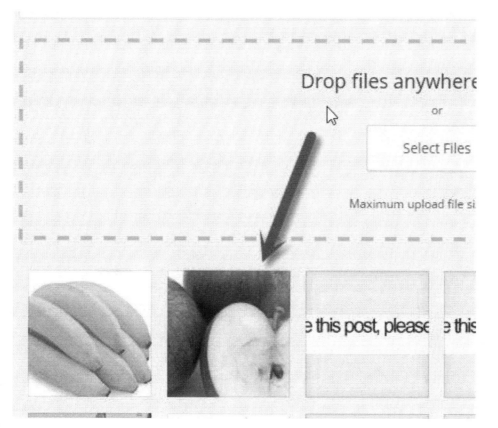

Clicking the thumbnail opens up this screen:

Attachment Details

< > ×

Edit Image

File name: apples-sections.jpg
File type: image/jpeg
Uploaded on: October 8, 2014
File size: 23 kB
Dimensions: 200 × 150

URL

http://rapidwpsites.c

Title

apples sections

Caption

Alt Text

Description

Uploaded By Andy Williams

You can change/add a caption, the title, ALT text (which is the text shown to people who have images turned off in their browsers, e.g. visually impaired or blind people who will have text to voice software in order to read the page contents), and the description.

You can also grab the **File URL** of your newly uploaded image. If you copy that and paste it into a web browser's address bar, the image will load in your browser.

We will look at how to add an image (or video), to a post later in this book. But for now, just try uploading a few images to get the hang of things. Once uploaded, grab the file URL and paste it into your browser. Do they load?

NOTE: There are some file formats that WordPress will not let you upload for security reasons. PHP files are one example. If you want to upload a file so that you can offer it as a download on your site, but it is not accepted for upload, then zip it up and upload the zipped file instead.

All of the media in your library can be viewed on the Media library screen:

Each item has the now familiar mouse-over menu, which allows you to Edit, Delete Permanently, or View that media item.

There is a column showing you the date the item was added to your library.

There is also a column called "Uploaded To". This column lets you know if that image was used on a post or page.

Note that columns in the media library are sortable by clicking the title of the column. Furthermore, if there are columns you don't use and don't want to see, you can hide them by using the screen options. Remember those?

Just unclick whichever items you don't want to see. You can even specify how many media items you see per page in your library.

If you have a lot of media in your library, there is a handy search feature:

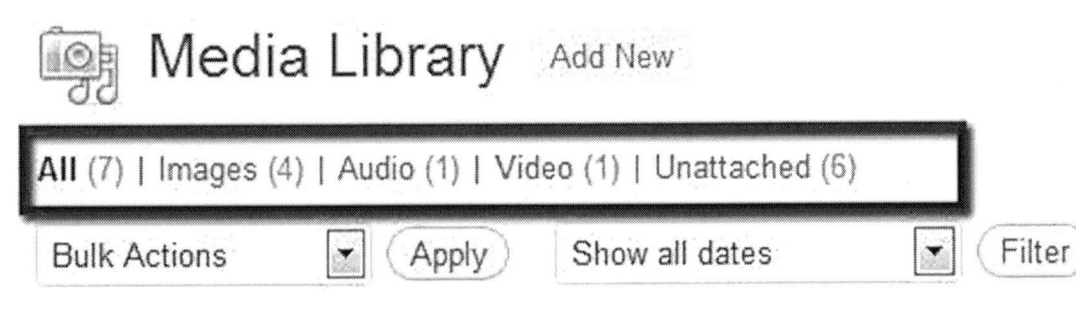

In the screenshot above, I searched for apples and the results returned the only media item called "apples". The search feature will look for your search text in both the title of the media and its description. If the word appears in either, it is shown in the search results.

Across the top of the media library, there are a few filtering options (depending on the types of media you have uploaded:

All (7) | Images (4) | Audio (1) | Video (1) | Unattached (6)

Bulk Actions ▾ (Apply)   Show all dates ▾ (Filter)

In the screenshot above, you can see there are 4 Images, 1 Audio file and 1 Video file. If I want to see just the images, I can click this images (4) link and just those items will be displayed in the media list. Similarly I can choose to just show audio or video.

Finally in the media library you have Bulk Actions (something that can be applied to multiple items in one go), and a further way to filter your media. I mention these together because they are found together on the screen:

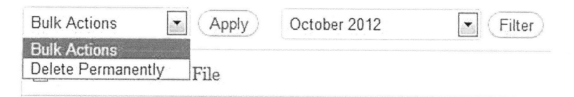

Next to each media item is a checkbox. If you want to delete several media items, you can check each one, and then select Delete Permanently from the Bulk Actions drop down box. Click Apply to delete the checked items.

To the right of that is a filter box that allows you to just view media that was uploaded in any particular month. Clicking on the drop down box only shows the months where media was uploaded, so just select the month of interest and click Filter. This is a great way of sorting through lots of media if you know you uploaded it last month, but cannot remember what it was called.

That's if for the Media Library for now. We will come back to this when we look at how to add content to your site using the What You See Is What You Get (WYSIWYG), document editor later.

Tasks to complete

1. Go and explore the media library. Practice uploading a photo, video or sound file and grabbing the URL.
2. Try using the search feature to find a specific piece of media in your library.

Pages v posts

When you want to add content to your site, you have two options. You can either create a new **Page** or a new **Post**. In terms of adding/editing, these two are very similar, but they are handled very differently by WordPress.

This may sound confusing to people who are new to WordPress (or maybe even new to website building). After all, isn't a post on your site a page? Doesn't a page on your site contain a post?

For some reason, WordPress creators decided to name these two types of content "posts" and "pages" and it does cause confusion. However, you DO need to understand the basic differences between them when it comes to building your site. The information I'll give you later will make it easy for you to decide which to use, so don't get hung up on these differences.

Since WordPress was originally designed as a blogging platform (i.e. to help build websites that were constantly updated with posts about whatever it was going on in that bloggers life), posts were designed for these regular updates.

WordPress posts are *date-dependent and chronological* and this separates them from Pages which are date-independent and not really related to any other piece of content on the site.

Posts were originally designed to be ordered by date, with a post you created yesterday logically appearing lower down the page than a post you make today. Newer posts are inserted at the top of the page, and older posts are pushed off the bottom.

It might help to think of an example.

Suppose you were keeping a blog about your weight loss program. On day one you weighed in at 210lb, so you write about that and what you have done for the day to help with your diet. Each day you write a new entry as a kind of personal journey on your weight loss progress.

When someone comes to your site, they see the daily posts in chronological order. This means visitors to your 'blog' can follow your story logically and see how your diet is working out for you.

This type of chronology is not possible to do with pages (well it is, but it takes a lot of effort plus plugins to achieve, so why bother?). Pages do not have any defined order within a site, though they can have a hierarchy with parent and child pages. We will look at this a little later on; so don't worry about it now.

OK, so the date-dependency is one important difference between WordPress posts and pages. What else?

142

Well, posts can be categorized, whereas pages cannot (at least not without plugins).

Suppose you were creating a site about exercise equipment. You might have a series of reviews on different treadmills, another set of reviews on exercise bikes, and so on.

Using posts allows us to categorize our content into relevant groups. If I had 10 reviews of various weight loss programs, I could create a category on my site called weight loss programs and add all 10 reviews to this category by writing them as posts.

Putting related content into the same category makes sense from a human visitor point of view, but also from the point of view of a search engine. If someone were on your site reading a review of the Hollywood Diet, it would be easy to take advantage of the features of posts in WordPress to also highlight some of the other diet reviews you have on your site. This can be done with posts (and we'll add a plugin called YARPP later to automate this), but it is a much more manual process if you tried doing the same thing with pages.

As well as categories, posts can also be tagged. Tags are an additional way to group and categorize your content. We'll discuss tags later, but for now, just realise that they can be used to further categorise your content to help your visitors and the search engines make sense of your project. It is possible to create tags for pages as well, but once again, only with plugins. However, we try not to use plugins unless they are absolutely essential as they do slow down the loading time of a website.

Another great feature of posts is that they can have **Excerpts**. These are short descriptions of the article that can be used by themes and plugins to create a Meta description tag, or a description of the article when linking to it. For example, below is a related posts section (created using the YARPP plugin that we'll install later), on one of my sites. It shows excerpts being used for the post descriptions:

Related Posts

1. EzSEO Newsletter – Createspace?
   Createspace is owned by Amazon and can take your PDF book and turn it into a physical book. There are a lot of things to learn though, so I am considering writing a series of tutorials in this newsletter. Does that interest you?

2. ezSEO Newsletter #347
   In this issue:
   1. A Couple of Useful Wordpress Plugins , 2. Email Software (and problems with Avast 8.0) , 3. Diagrams, Mind Maps and More , 4. Kindle Bestselles Secrets, 5. Both SEO Books in a Single Volume

3. EzSEO Newsletter #345
   TweetIn this issue: 1. Moving WordPress Posts to Another Site 2. New SEO Tips Videos 3. Where to promote your Kindle books Hi Again In this newsletter I've got a few video tutorials for you, plus some help for those of you starting out with Kindle . Incidentally, one reader told me they had their [...]

4. Kindle Sales Update
   Kindle Publishing. Does it really work? Here are my sales figures so far.

Without excerpts, the first X words of the article itself are used for the description (see item 3 in the screenshot above). This looks untidy since it finishes mid-sentence and uses a double or triple period (...) to signify that there is more to read. Also, bear in mind that the first sentence or two of the article does not always make the best description for the article.

Another important feature of posts is that they appear in your site's RSS feed. Remember, we talked about how important that was earlier in the book. Since RSS feeds are there to highlight the most recent posts, any important new content on the site should be a post so that it can be seen in your feeds.

One of the original differences between pages and posts was that pages could use different templates whereas posts could not. This meant that different pages on your site might have totally different layouts. This was not possible with posts. However, with the introduction of WordPress 3.1, a feature called **Post Formats** was introduced. We will look at this feature briefly when we add a post to the site, but for now, understand that post formats allow you to change the layout of your posts by selecting from a list of formats.

When to use posts and when to use pages

Not all webmasters agree on this, but I am going to give you a simple rule that will tell you when to use a post and when to use a page. This is the way I have built WordPress sites for myself and my clients for several years, and the system offers great SEO benefits as well as organizing content in a logical manner to help both

144

visitors and search engines.

Before I tell you the rule, let me first distinguish between two types of content that you may have on your site.

The first type of content is that which is important to your niche and you want visitors to see. We will call this type of content, **Niche Content**. This will include all articles, reviews, etc. that you write for your site and your targeted audience.

The second type of content is that which you don't really care whether visitors see or not. The only reason we put it on the site is because we need to include it for various purposes. This type of content is frequently unrelated to any other. Typical examples would be a Privacy page, Terms of Service, Contact page, and an About Us page (although a good 'About Us' page is one exception that we should make visible to our visitors). Apart from the About Us page, these others types of pages are what I call **Legal Pages**, since the only reason they are on the site is because we are required to have them there by law, or to comply with search engine rules.

OK, you get the difference?

Here is the basic rule.

Use Posts for Niche (topical), Content, and Pages for Legal Content.

Simple enough, but I am sure some of you may still not quite get it. You will when we start adding pages and posts to the website. Before we can do that though, we need to look at post categories and tags.

Tasks to complete

1. Go over this section until the differences between pages and posts are clear in your mind.

Categories & tags

Before we can start adding posts to our site, we need to think about the way the site will be structured and how the posts will be organized within the site itself.

We have already touched on categories and tags earlier in the book, and have set up the SEO settings for these taxonomies (organization of content). Let's now have a closer look at categories and tags so that you can fully understand them and add a few to your own site.

Both categories and tags are ways to categorize your posts.

All posts MUST be assigned to a category, but posts DO NOT have to have tags assigned to them. In that respect, categories are more important than tags.

Think of categories as the main way to categorize your posts, and tags as a further way to provide even more details about your posts.

Let's look at an example.

Let's consider a website about vacuum cleaners. What would the main categories be on a website about vacuum cleaners?

To think about this in a different way, how would you want to group the articles on your vacuum cleaner site so that related articles were in the same category?

Here are some ideas:

Dyson

Handheld

Dyson Ball

Eureka

Bagless

Cordless

Hoover

Upright

Canister

Miele

HEPA filter

All of these could be categories, but then you might get to the situation where one post might fit into several categories. While WordPress encourages this, I recommend you put each post into ONE category only. Thinking about one category per post actually helps you find the best categories for your site.

Of those ideas listed above, which ones would make the most sense if a vacuum could only be in one category?

How about "bagless"?

Nope. A vacuum could be bagless, upright and a Dyson.

The obvious categories from those listed above would be the categories that would only allow a post to be in one category - the brand names. My categories would therefore be:

Dyson

Eureka

Hoover

Miele

A Dyson DC25 vacuum cleaner review could only go in one category – the Dyson category.

So what about the other terms:

Handheld

Dyson Ball

Bagless

Cordless

Upright

Canister

HEPA filter

Well, these are perfect as tags because they add a little more information/detail about the post. For example, my review of the Dyson DC25 vacuum would be in the category Dyson, but could be tagged with ball, HEPA, bagless & upright.

The beauty (and danger), of using tags is that for every tag you use, WordPress will create a page just for that tag. In the example above, WordPress would create FOUR tag pages. One for "ball", one for "HEPA", one for "Bagless" and one for "Upright".

The "HEPA" tag page will list all vacuums on the site that have been tagged with HEPA - it helps visitors find more HEPA vacuums if that is what they are interested in.

The "Bagless" tag page would list all vacuums on the site that were bagless (and therefore tagged with that term). A visitor on my site looking for a bagless vacuum could use the tag page to quickly see all available bagless vacuums that had been reviewed to date.

These tags also give search engines indications about our content, helping them understand what it's about so that it can rank better for related searches.

Tags are powerful. However, with that power comes some responsibility.

If you abuse tags, your site will become spammy. I have seen sites where posts have been tagged with 10, 20, 50, and even several hundred tags. Don't believe me? See this screenshot showing the tags for a post on one website I came across:

You don't need to be able to read the words in that screenshot to get the point. I've had to reduce the size of the screenshot to get all the tags into view. There are over 160 tags for that one article, and by the way, I happen to know that Google penalised this particular site.

Think about the problems of tag abuse by thinking how WordPress works and how it handles tags.

Every tag in that list will have its own tag page.

The biggest problem for that site is that many of the tags used on that post are not used on any other posts. That means there are 100+ tag pages with just a single post listed as using that tag.

To think about this in another way, if that was the only post on the site, there would be over 160 pages on it.

The way the webmaster used tags in this example is what Google would call "spam". Please, use tags responsibly!

Let's look at one more example.

Think of a recipe website about puddings, desserts, cakes and so on.

You might have main categories like:

Ice cream

Cakes

Muffins

Mousse

Cookies

These are the obvious categories since a dessert will only be able to fit into one of the categories. To further classify the recipes on the site, we'd use tags which would add a little more detail about each post.

What type of tags would you use?

Stuck for ideas?

Tags become more apparent when you look at a particular recipe. If the recipe was for chocolate brownies, then the category would be cakes and maybe you'd have tags like chocolate, walnuts, frosting. See how those tags compliment the category in helping to classify the recipe?

Those tags would be used on other posts too, e.g. banana cake (at least the way my mama makes it), would also be tagged with frosting and walnuts.

Chocolate would probably be a common tag in dessert recipes. Think of chocolate chip ice cream, chocolate mousse, chocolate gateaux, etc.

Do you see how the tags help define the article, giving a little more description about the contents of the piece? This is the mindset you are looking to develop as you utilize tags for your own website.

A few guidelines for using tags

1. Keep a list of tags you use on your site and make sure you spell them correctly when you reuse them. Remember, if you misspell a tag, another tag page will be created for the misspelt version.

2. Don't create tags that will only apply to one post. Remember, tags are there to help classify your content into groups. Most tags will be used several times on a site, and its use will increase as you add more content.

3. Only pick a small number of relevant tags per post. I'd recommend somewhere between 3 – 6 tags per post, but if some need more, then that's fine. If some need less that's OK too. This is just a general rule of thumb.

4. NEVER use a tag that is also a category.

Setting up categories & tags in your dashboard

Categories and tags are properties of posts, so you'll find the menus to work with them under the Posts menu of the Dashboard navigation.

Categories and tags can either be set up before you start writing content, or added as you are composing it. The most common method is to set up categories before you begin, but add tags while you are writing your post.

I recommend that you create a description for all tags and categories, and to do that, you will need to go into the pages using the links in this menu.

OK, let's go and set up a category first. Click on the categories menu:

On the right you will see a list of any existing categories. There is only one – uncategorized, that WordPress has set up for you. Since this is the default category on the site (See Writing Settings), we want to change this to be a default category and one that means something to our site. If you mouse over the category title, you'll get the menu appear underneath it:

	Name	Description	Slug	Posts
☐	Uncategorized Edit | Quick Edit | View		uncategorized	2
☐	Name	Description	Slug	Posts

Bulk Actions ▾ (Apply)   *1 item*

The Quick Edit will allow you to change the category name AND the category slug.

The slug is just the text that is used in the URL to represent the category of the post. Remember we set up Permalinks earlier to look like this:

/%category%/%postname%/

The %category% variable is replaced by the category slug and the %postname% variable will be replaced by the post name slug.

To create the category slug, WordPress uses the same text as the category name (converted to lowercase), with any spaces bridged by a dash.

Therefore a category name of **juicer reviews** would have a default slug of **juicer-reviews**, but you can specify your own slug if you prefer not to use the WordPress default.

Since we want to add a description to every category we create (to be used as the category Meta description), we need to click on the **Edit** link to give us access to all settings for that category.

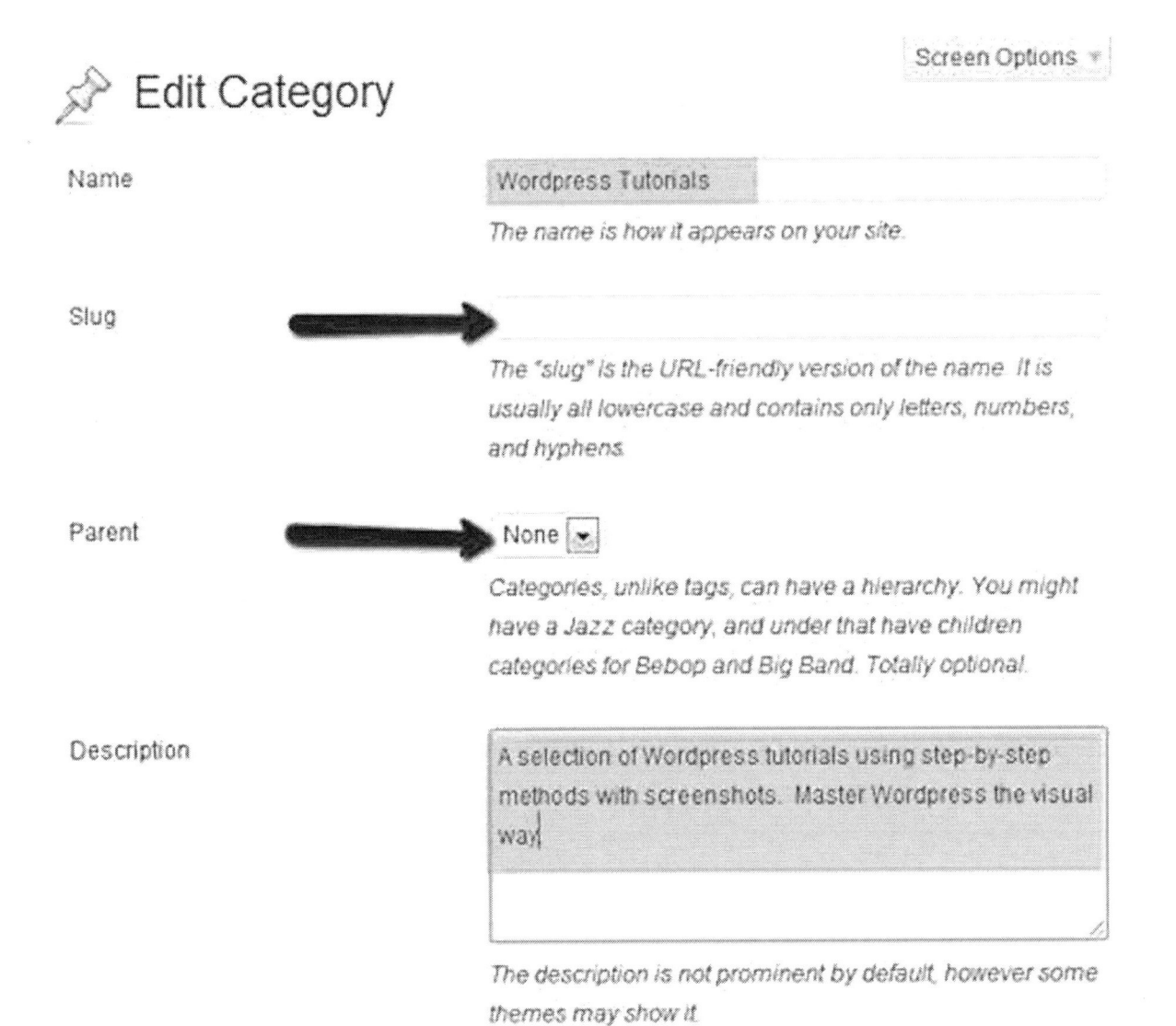

Edit Category

Name

Wordpress Tutorials

The name is how it appears on your site.

Slug

The "slug" is the URL-friendly version of the name. It is usually all lowercase and contains only letters, numbers, and hyphens.

Parent

None ▾

Categories, unlike tags, can have a hierarchy. You might have a Jazz category, and under that have children categories for Bebop and Big Band. Totally optional.

Description

A selection of Wordpress tutorials using step-by-step methods with screenshots. Master Wordpress the visual way

The description is not prominent by default, however some themes may show it.

I have entered a new category name for my default category (the default is the one that is selected when you create a new post). You can of course change this by selecting a different category as appropriate.

I have left the slug empty. When I save these settings, WordPress will use **wordpress-tutorials** as the slug. Therefore the URLs of the posts in this category will look like this:

http://visualwordpress.com/wordpress-tutorials/installing-plugins

I have added a description that will be used as the Meta description of the category page, but I have not selected a parent category.

NOTE: If you have installed the Wordpress SEO plugin by Yoast, you will have more options on your category edit screen. We will look at these in a moment.

Parent categories & hierarchy

Categories can be hierarchical. In other words, you can have categories within categories.

An example might be a website on car maintenance. I might have a category called Toyota, but then want sub-categories called Engine, Brakes, and Exhaust etc.

Therefore the parent category would be Toyota. When I create the engine, brake & exhaust categories, I'd select Toyota as the parent.

Add New Category

Name

```
Engine
```

The name is how it appears on your site.

Slug

The "slug" is the URL-friendly version of the name. It is usually all lowercase and contains only letters, numbers, and hyphens.

Parent

```
Toyota                ▼
```

Categories, unlike tags, can have a hierarchy. You might have a Jazz category, and under that have children categories for Bebop and Big Band. Totally optional.

Description

```
Maintenance of the Toyota car engine.
```

The description is not prominent by default; however, some themes may show it.

In the list of categories you can spot parent/child relationships within categories because they are shown in the table as a line next to the child. The child is indented:

☐	Name	Description
☐	Toyota	
☐	— Brakes	
☐	— Exhaust	
☐	— Engine	Maintenance of the Toyota car engine.

On my website, I could then have a menu item called Toyota, which opens up when you mouse over to include the child categories.

Toyota	
Brakes	
Engine	ısdf ɛ
Exhaust	ısdf ɛ
	sdf ɛ

Parent – Child categories are very useful for tidying up the categorization on your site.

Imagine if you had 10 brands of cars, and 10 different areas on maintenance for each type of car. That would require 100 categories which would be too many to display on a website. By using parent-child categories, you can just have the 10 brands as the parent categories on your site, with the maintenance sections only visible on mouse-over as children to the parents.

Adding a new category

Adding a new category is easy. Fill in the title, slug (if you want to), and a description. Then select a parent if applicable. Click the **Add New Category** button and your new category is ready for use.

If you go to the category list and click the Edit link of a category, you'll actually notice more settings than just Title, Slug, Parent and Category. These additional settings are only seen when you go into full edit mode, and they are added there by the WordPress SEO plugin by Yoast that we set up earlier.

Here are those WordPress SEO Plugin settings:

Yoast WordPress SEO Settings

SEO Title:

The SEO title is used on the archive page for this term.

SEO Description:

The SEO description is used for the meta description on the archive page for this term.

Canonical:

The canonical link is shown on the archive page for this term.

Breadcrumbs Title:

The Breadcrumbs title is used in the breadcrumbs where this category appears.

Noindex this category: Use category default (Currently: index) ▾

Include in sitemap?:   Auto detect ▾

You can actually ignore these settings because WordPress does a good enough job of handling categories. There is only one setting here that is worth thinking about now, which is the **Noindex this category** drop down box.

Noindex this category: Use category default (Currently: index) ▾

Include in sitemap?:   Use category default (Currently: index)
Always index
Always noindex

This allows you to set up some categories to be **noindex** with the search engines. Although this isn't something you normally want to do, it does highlight the fine level of control that this plugin adds to WordPress. We'll see more of this fine level of control when we add new content later.

Adding Tags is very similar to adding categories except tags cannot have a parent child relationship with each other.

For every tag you enter, add a description to explain what that tag is being used for. That description will then be used for the Meta description of the tag page; this is how we set it up within the SEO plugin, remember?

Similar to the categories, the **Add Tag** screen has just a few options – Title, Slug and Description. You only need to fill in the Title and Description because WordPress will handle the slug for us. However, if you go in and edit an existing tag, you will see extra Yoast WordPress SEO plugin settings for the tag. Again, these can be ignored for now, because WordPress handles tags very well.

While I expect you will add tags directly on the **Add Post** screen as you write your content, I do highly recommend you come back to this section every time you use a new tag, just to fill in a description for those tags you create. When you make a new tag on the **Add Post** screen, you don't have the option of adding the description there and then, but it is important to add one nonetheless.

Tasks to complete

1. Set up a few categories for your site.
2. Think about possible tags and keep a list on a notepad.
3. Make sure to add descriptions to every tag and category that you add.

Writing posts

Whether you are writing posts or pages, the main content editor is the same.

To create a new post on your site, click the Posts -> Add New link in the Dashboard navigation menu.

The Add Post (and Add Page) screen has a lot of information on it. Let's look at the What You See Is What You Get (WYSIWYG) Editor first.

WordPress WYSIWYG editor

The toolbar of the editor (the place where you add your content), looks like this:

You'll see on the top right there are two tabs – Visual & Text (the Text tab was called the HTML tab in previous versions of WordPress).

The Visual tab is where you can write your content using WYSIWYG features. On this tab you'll see text and media formatted as it will appear on the website once published. This is the tab you will want to use for most of the work you do when adding new, or editing existing content, on your site.

The other tab – Text - shows the raw code that is responsible for the layout and content of the page. Unless you specifically need to insert some code or script into your content, stick with the Visual tab.

On the toolbar, the button at the far right (see screenshot above), opens up more features (tool buttons), of the toolbar. Some of the features are well worth using, so click on that button. Your toolbar will now look like this:

The two rows of buttons allow you to format your content visually. If you have used any type of Word Processor before, then this should be fairly intuitive.

I won't go through the functions of all these buttons. If you want to see what each one does, move your mouse over it and you'll get a toolbar tip appear giving details.

Adding content to your site is as easy as typing it into the large box under the toolbar.

As you write your content you can select text and then click a toolbar button to format the selected word(s). Make it bold, or change its colour, make it a header, or any of the other features offered in the toolbar.

You can easily create headlines from the drop down box (far left, bottom row) on the toolbar. Write the headline, select it with your mouse, and choose the header you want from the drop down box:

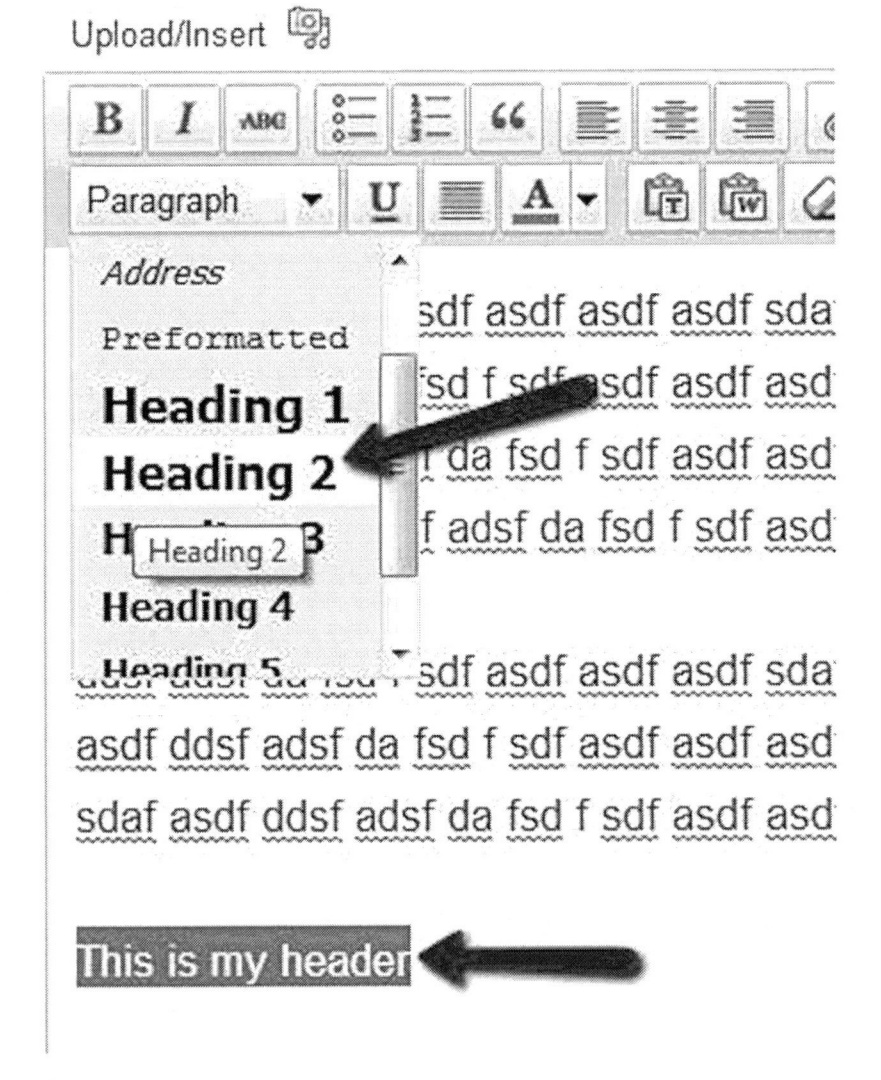

NOTE:

WordPress templates typically show the title of your post as an H1 header at the top of the page. This is the biggest header available and is equivalent to the **Heading1** in

158

the drop down selector. You should not use more than one H1 header in your article, so DO NOT use any **Heading 1** headers as you write your content. Use **Heading 2** for sections of your article, and **Heading 3** for sub-headers inside **Heading 2** sections of your content.

OK, it's now time to go ahead and write an article (post), for your website.

As you write your article, you may want to insert an image or some other form of media. We looked at the Media library earlier in the book, but let's now go through the process of adding an image to an article we are currently working on.

Adding images

Position your cursor in the article where you want to add the image. Don't worry too much about getting it in the right place because you can always re-position it later if you need to.

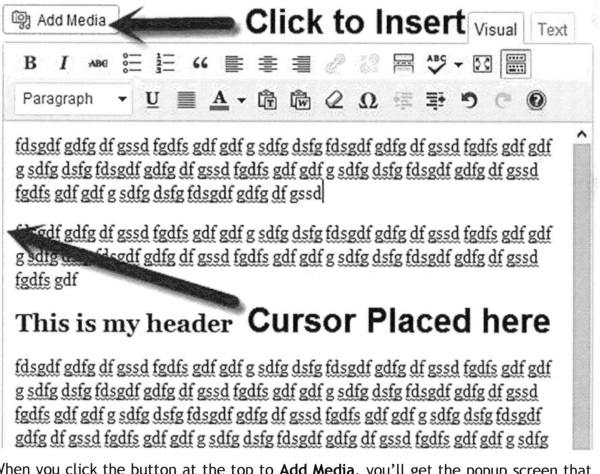

When you click the button at the top to **Add Media**, you'll get the popup screen that we've seen previously:

Insert Media

Insert Media

Create Gallery

Set Featured Image

Insert from URL

Upload Files   Media Library

Drop files anywhere to upload

Select Files

Maximum upload file size: 64MB

Insert into post

From this screen you can upload an image (or other media), from your computer by dragging-and-dropping it into the main rectangle containing the **Select Files** button. You can also add from a URL, or preselect a file from your Media library.

Let's add an image from our Media Library that we uploaded earlier. Click the Media Library tab on this screen.

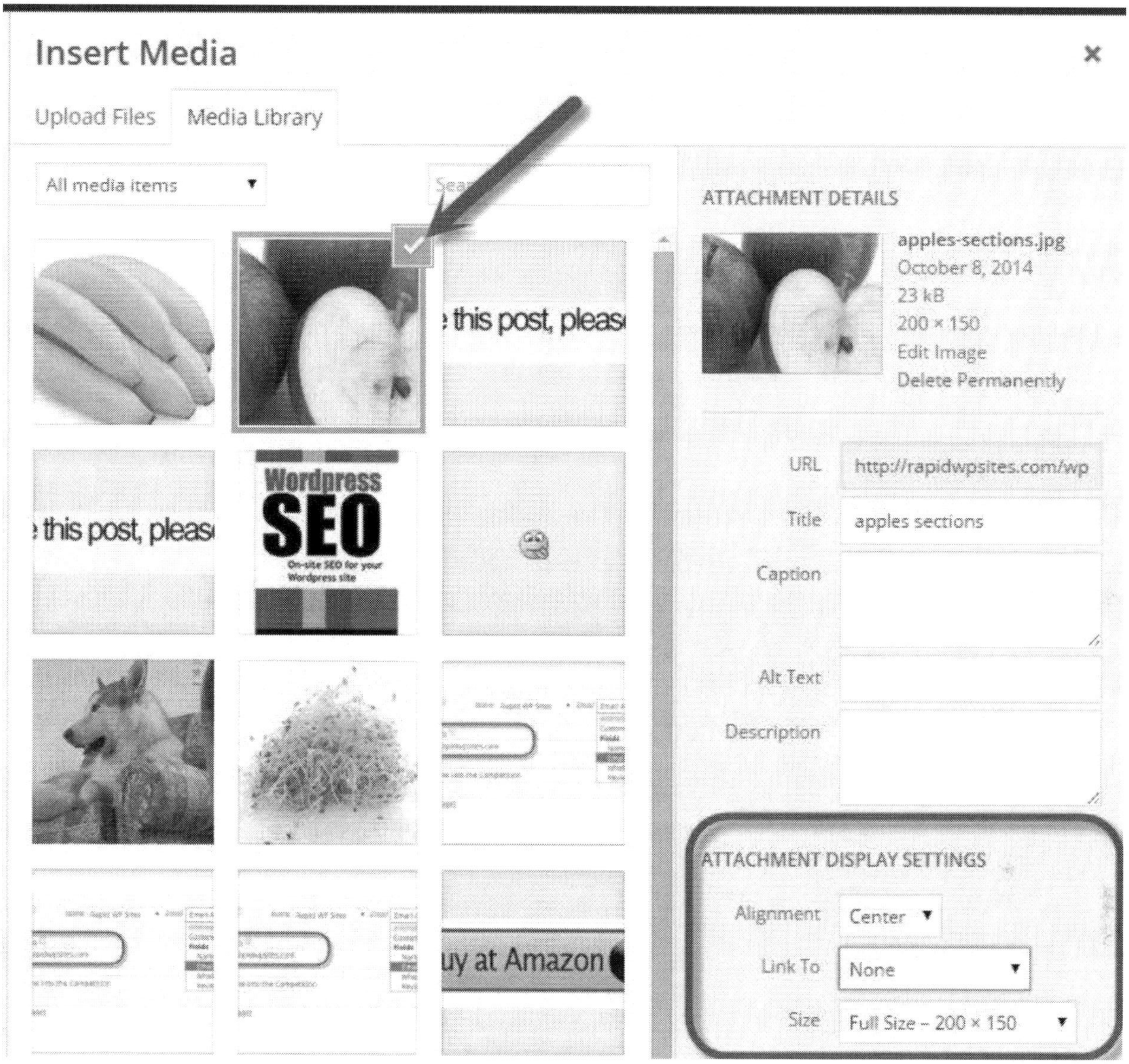

Insert Media

Upload Files   Media Library

All media items ▼   Sea

ATTACHMENT DETAILS

apples-sections.jpg
October 8, 2014
23 kB
200 × 150
Edit Image
Delete Permanently

URL   http://rapidwpsites.com/wp

Title   apples sections

Caption

Alt Text

Description

ATTACHMENT DISPLAY SETTINGS

Alignment   Center ▼

Link To   None ▼

Size   Full Size – 200 × 150 ▼

When you click on the image you want to insert, a check mark appears in the top right corner. The image details are shown on the right side, and can be edited (Title, Caption, ALT text, Description, Alignment & Size).

At the bottom of the right hand column are some display settings. Currently my image is set to be aligned "Center". I want my image aligned left, so need to select **Left** from the Alignment drop-down box.

Note that if you select an alignment for your image, the text will wrap around that image. If you leave it at the default **None**, then there is no wrapping of text around the image.

The next option you have is to link your image to something. The default setting is

"Media File", which means the image will open in a new browser tab when clicked. That's not what you generally want, so select "None". That means the image does not link to anything. One useful option here is to link your image to a Custom URL. For example, if your image is a "Buy Now" button, you'd want the image linked to the purchase page.

The last of the display settings is "Size". You'll be able to choose from Full size and thumbnail (possibly other sizes like medium).

I also want my image size to be full size, so I'd select **Full Size** from the size drop-down box.

Once I have made my selection, I click the **Insert into post** button at the bottom.

Here is that image inserted into my post at the position of my cursor:

fdsgdf gdfg df gssd fgdfs gdf gdf g sdfg dsfg fdsgdf gdfg df gssd fgdfs gdf gdf g sdfg dsfg g sdfg dsfg fdsgdf gdfg df gssd fgdfs gdf gdf g sdfg dsfg fdsgdf gdfg df gssd

fdsgdf gdfg df gssd fgdfs gdf gdf g sd gdf gdf g sdfg dsfg fdsgdf gdfg df gss fdsgdf gdfg df gssd fgdfs gdf

This is my header

fdsgdf gdfg df gssd fgdfs gdf gdf g sd gdf gdf g sdfg dsfg fdsgdf gdfg df gss fdsgdf gdfg df gssd fgdfs gdf gdf g sd gdf gdf g sdfg dsfg fdsgdf gdfg df gss fdsgdf gdfg df gssd fgdfs gdf gdf g sd gdf gdf g sdfg dsfg fdsgdf gdfg df gss

If you have the position wrong, you can simply click and drag the image to a different location.

If you find that the image isn't inserted as you intended (e.g. you forgot to align it so don't have word-wrap), click on the image and two buttons will appear. The one on the right will delete the image so that you can start again, and the one on the left will re-open the properties screen so you can edit the image properties as required.

Click the button on the left to open the properties screen:

Image Details

Caption

Alternative Text: Pile Of Fresh Alfalfa Sprouts

DISPLAY SETTINGS

Align | Left | Center | Right | None

Size | Full Size – 200 × 170 ▾

Link To | Media File ▾

http://rapidwpsites.com/wp-content/up

Edit Original   Replace

ADVANCED OPTIONS ▲

Update

Notice that on the left, there is a **Size** drop down box. This offers you a thumbnail or full size image, or a **Custom Size** which allows you to enter the exact dimensions you want.

Below these settings you'll see some **Advanced Settings**:

ADVANCED OPTIONS ▲

Image Title Attribute

Image CSS Class

☐ Open link in a new window/tab

Link Rel

Link CSS Class

One advanced feature that you may find useful is the check box to "Open link in a new window/tab". This is useful when your image links to another web page and you want that link to open in a new browser window.

You can insert videos from your Media library in exactly the same way.

OK, now go on to finish your first post.

There are a few things we need to do before we make our article live. Let's go through the complete sequence from start, to publish:

1. Add a title.
2. Write & format your post using the visual text editor (WYSIWYG).
3. Select a post format if available.
4. Select a category.
5. Add some tags.
6. Add an excerpt.
7. Select a date/time if you want to schedule the post for the future.
8. Publish/Schedule the post.

OK, so we have completed down to step 2.

Post format

Not all WordPress themes use Post Formats. The Twenty Eleven theme that we are using does, so let's look at what these post formats are. On the right of your screen you see the Format options.

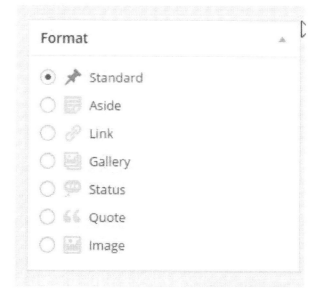

Since most, if not all of your posts, should use the default (Standard format), we won't go into details in this book about other formats. Most people just won't use them and not all templates support them. If you are interested in post formats, experiment with them and then view your post to see how it looks. You can also read more about Post Formats on the WordPress websites:

http://codex.wordpress.org/Post_Formats

The next step in our publishing sequence is to choose a category. Choose just one category for each post. You can add a new category "on the fly" from within the Add post screen, but if you do, remember to go in and write a description for the new category so it can be used as the meta description of that category page (remember the WordPress SEO plugin we set up earlier is expecting a description for categories and tags).

Select 3-5 tags for the post. Add your chosen tags to a list that you maintain so you can reuse (with correct spellings), those tags on other posts. You can enter tags, even if they don't already exist, simply by typing them into the tag box. When you are finished, click the **Add** button to the right of the tags box.

Tags ▼

tag1, tag2, tag3| (Add)

Separate tags with commas

Choose from the most used tags

As you add and use more tags, you can click on the link **Choose from the most used tags** and a box will appear with some of the tags you've used before. You can just click the tags that apply, and they'll be added to the tag list of your post.

If you add "new" tags when entering a post, I recommend you go into the Tags settings to write a short description for each one. Yes it takes time. However, this will be used as the Meta description of the tag page because we set this up using the WordPress SEO plugin earlier.

Next up is adding an excerpt to your post. This should be a short description that you want to show your visitors. Its purpose is to encourage them to click through and read the article. This excerpt will be used as the Meta description tag of the post, as well as the description of the post in the "related posts" section, which is displayed at the end of each article you publish (see the YARPP plugin later).

To enter the excerpt, scroll down below the WYSIWYG editor until you find the box labeled excerpts: If you do not see it, click the screen options button on the top right, and make sure the excerpts box is checked. While you are in the screen options, I recommend you check ALL of the boxes. As you work out what you need and what you don't, you can uncheck those that are not of interest.

Excerpt

Excerpts are optional hand-crafted summaries of your content that can be used in your theme. Learn more about manual excerpts.

Enter a three to five sentence paragraph to encourage the click.

OK, the next step in the process is deciding when you want the post to go live on your site. If you want it up there immediately, then click the Publish button. If, like me, you are writing several posts in a batch, it is a good idea to spread the posting of the content out a little bit. Luckily, WordPress allows us to schedule the posts into the future.

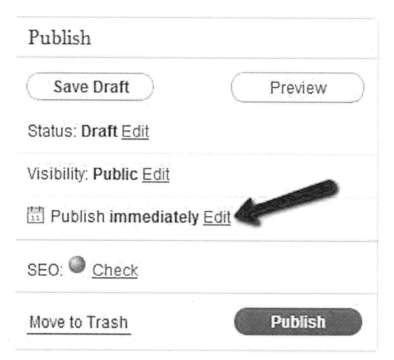

In the Publish box over on the right side, the default is to publish **immediately**. However, there is an Edit link that you can click which opens up a calendar for scheduling:

Enter the date and time you want to publish the post and then click the OK button.

The publish button now changes to Schedule.

Click the Schedule button to schedule the post.

That's it. You've just published or scheduled your first WordPress post.

Before we move on, there is one last thing to cover here. It's the way that the WordPress SEO plugin we installed earlier is integrated into the Add Post (and Add Page), screen.

If you scroll down a little, you should come across the **WordPress SEO by Yoast** section.

NOTE: If you don't see this section, make sure it is checked in the screen options (top right).

There are 4 tabs across the top of these settings. You can ignore the **General** tab as we have already entered a title and Meta description (the excerpt). The **Focus Keyword** can also be ignored. It was useful in the past when optimizing a web page, but today, that kind of thing can easily get you into trouble with Google.

Similarly, ignore the **Page Analysis** tab as that relates to optimization of the web page for your focus keyword. You'll only end up in trouble using this.

The important settings that we might be interested in are on the Advanced tab, and even then, only the ones at the top of that section:

General   Page Analysis   Advanced   Social

Meta Robots Index: Default for post type, currently: index ▼

Meta Robots Follow: ⦿ Follow ○ Nofollow

Meta Robots Advanced: None
                          NO ODP
                          NO YDIR
                          No Archive
                          No Snippet

Advanced meta robots settings for this page.

Include in Sitemap: Auto detect ▼

Should this page be in the XML Sitemap at all times,

I have highlighted the only settings you really need to know for now.

These settings give us fine control over how the search engines will deal with this post. Not all posts, just THIS post. With this fine level of control, we can treat every post and page on our site differently if we want to.

The top setting is Meta Robot Index. The default settings were set up when we installed the plugin. Essentially we want ALL posts to be indexed. If we want to make a particular post noindex, we can do it here with that top drop down box.

The next setting is whether we want links on the post followed. Default is yes but we can set them to nofollow. I don't recommend changing this unless you know what you are doing.

The Meta Robots Advanced allows us to set a few other Meta tags on our pages.

No ODP and No YDIR can be ignored.

No Archive tag tells Google not to store a cached copy of your page

No Snippet tells Google not to show a description under your Google listing (nor will it show a cached link in the search results).

The only one you may want to use here is the No Archive option, but only in very special circumstances. There are times when we don't want Google to keep an archive (cached version), of a page. We can set the Meta tag to say No Archive for any post or page with these settings, thereby preventing the search engines from keeping a backup of the page.

Why might you want to do this? Well, maybe you have a limited offer on your site and you don't want people seeing it after the offer has finished. If the page was archived, it is technically possible for someone to go in and see the last cached page at Google, which will still show your previous offer.

The social tab of these settings can also be ignored. It might be something you want to look into when your site takes off though.

Editing posts

At some point, after you have written a post, you may want to go in and edit or update it. This is an easy process. Just click on the **All Posts** link in the **Posts** menu. It will open a screen with a list of posts on your site.

Now it's just a question of how to find the actual post you want to update or edit. There are two ways of doing this. One is from within your Dashboard using the available search and filtering tools. The other method is one I'll show you later by visiting your website while you are logged into the Dashboard.

For now, let's look at how we can find posts from within the Dashboard:

Firstly, if you know what month you wrote the post, you could show all posts from that month. I don't use that feature as it's easier using other methods.

Alternatively, you can search for a post by showing just those posts within a certain category. You can do this by selecting the category you want to search from the "View all Categories" drop down box at the top.

Perhaps the easiest way of all is to use the Search Posts feature. Type in a keyword phrase you know is in the title, and then click the **Search Posts** button.

Once the list of matching posts is displayed, mouse over the one you want to edit to bring its menu into view, and select edit. Or, a simpler way is to just click the title of the post.

This takes you back to the same editor screen you used when first creating the post. Make your changes in there and just click the **Update** button to save your modifications.

NOTE: Whenever you make changes to a post, WordPress keeps a record (archive), of those changes. At the bottom of your Add/Edit post screen is a section called **Revisions**. If you don't see it, make sure it is checked in the screen options from the top.

Revisions

18 June, 2013 @ 10:27 by Andy Williams

17 June, 2013 @ 14:05 by Andy Williams

17 June, 2013 @ 14:02 by Andy Williams

17 June, 2013 @ 13:51 by Andy Williams

17 June, 2013 @ 13:46 by Andy Williams

17 June, 2013 @ 12:40 by Andy Williams

17 June, 2013 @ 12:36 by Andy Williams

17 June, 2013 @ 12:35 by Andy Williams

17 June, 2013 @ 12:34 by Andy Williams

17 June, 2013 @ 12:30 by Andy Williams

17 June, 2013 @ 12:28 by Andy Williams

17 June, 2013 @ 12:27 by Andy Williams

You can view any previous version of the post by clicking the date link. This does not lose the current contents; it just opens a viewer screen where you can see what that version looked like:

Revision for "Hello world!" created on 15 October, 2012 @ 7:10

Title

    Hello world!

Content

    Welcome to WordPress. This is your first post. Edit or delete it, then start blogging!

Excerpt

Revisions

Compare Revisions

Old	New	Date Created	Author	Actions
○	⦿	24 October, 2012 @ 11:32 [Current Revision]	Andy Williams	
○	○	24 October, 2012 @ 18:04 [Autosave]	Andy Williams	Restore
○	○	23 October, 2012 @ 14:53	Andy Williams	Restore

At the very top you can see the revision you are looking at. It will be the revision you clicked on in the previous screen. The content of that revision is highlighted in yellow in my screenshot. This is the content of the post for that date.

You can also see further down there's a list of all revisions with the currently published revision selected. You can view the contents of any revision simply by clicking on it in the list. The preview will appear at the top of the screen.

What is useful is the **Compare Revisions** button. This will compare a currently published version with the revision you are previewing.

```
Welcome to WordPress. This is
your first post. Edit or
delete it, then start
blogging!
```

```
    Welcome to WordPress. This is your
  + first post. Edit or delete it, then
    start blogging! ;-)

  + http://youtu.be/YersIyzsOpc

    <a href="http://com-vip.org/?
    attachment_id=34"><img
    class="alignnone size-full wp-
    image-34" title="apples"
  + src="http://com-vip.org/wp-
    content/uploads/2012/10/apples.jpg"
    alt="" width="284" height="221" />
    </a>

  +  
```

At the top of each revision is the title. The one on the right is also labeled as the "Current Revision". This is the one that is published live on your site. The older version is on the left.

If you decide you want to revert back to an earlier version, you can click the **Restore** link next to the version you want to return to. WordPress won't ask for confirmation before restoring the old version, but it doesn't matter. If you make a mistake, just return back to the list and restore the one you actually wanted.

Tasks to complete

1. Enter a post. It doesn't have to be real post and you can always delete it afterwards. I just want you to get used to writing content in the WYSIWYG editor. So add text and an image, and then play around with the image alignment and settings.

2. Publish your post and go to your site to see how it looks in your web browser.

3. Go back and edit the post.

4. Now scroll to the bottom of the page and look at the revisions section. Check out the differences between two different versions of your post, and try reinstating an older version. Then change it back to show the later post again.

Making it easy for visitors to socially share your content

Having great content on your site is one thing, but getting people to see it is something else.

One of the ways people find a website is through the search engines. They search for something and Google shows them the most relevant links. If we rank well enough for a particular search term, the web searcher may land on our page.

Another way people can find our content is via social media channels. Places like Facebook, Google plus, and Twitter are good examples. To make this more likely, we need to install a social sharing plugin on the site. A social sharing plugin will add buttons to the website that allow people to share the content they are reading by the simple click of a mouse. Social sharing buttons make sharing easy, and therefore more likely.

There are a number of great social sharing plugins, so you can actually choose whichever one you want. The one I recommend you start off with is called **Add Twitter, Facebook Like, Google plus one Social share**.

Search the plugins for that and you'll find it:

Add Twitter, Facebook Like, Google plus one Social share

Install Now

More Details

WordPress plugin for twitter, facebook, Google +1 (plus one) and other social share. Can add the share box before post contents, after and also floati

By Kunal Chichkar

★★★☆ (98)

330,122 downloads

Last Updated: 6 months ago

Untested with your version of WordPress

Install and activate the plugin. You'll then find the settings for the plugin inside the main **Settings** menu.

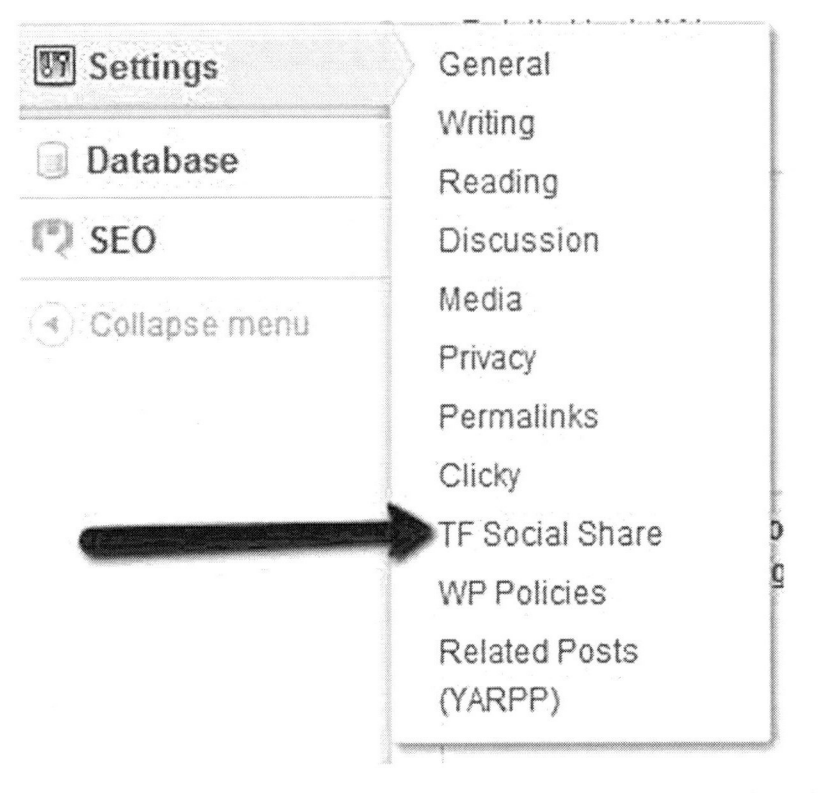

Go to the settings menu so we can access and setup the plugin.

Let's go through these settings bit by bit. At the top you can define which buttons you want to appear on your site:

Facebook and Twitter share buttons

General options		
Auto Display:	☑ *Enable Auto display of Social Share buttons at specified postion*	
Code for Manual Display:	`<?php if(function_exists('kc_add_social_share')) kc_add_social_share(); ?>`	
Active share buttons:	☑ Facebook like ☑ Stumbleupon ☐ LinkedIn	☑ Twitter ☑ Google PlusOne ☐ Pinterest
Show buttons in these pages:	☑ Single posts ☑ Home page ☑ Categories ☐ Search results	☐ Pages ☑ Tags ☐ Author archives ☐ Archives

You can select whichever ones you want. I don't typically select Pinterest unless my site has a lot of images that I want shared. I also don't include LinkedIn unless the site is more business orientated.

Once you select which buttons to show, you can then select where to share them. I'd recommend you put them on any post or page you want shared. That means **single posts**, **home page**, **categories** & **tags**.

Before we move onto the next set of options, make sure that the **Auto Display** check box is checked at the top.

OK, next we decide where on our content the buttons should appear. I usually choose above and below, but you can play around with these settings and decide on something you like.

Note:	*Left Floating is available only for single post and Static pages. By Default the bar will be displayed above the post.*
Position:	Above and Below the post ▾
Border Style:	No Border ▾
Show Background Color:	☐
Background Color:	#F0F4F9 *Default Color wont disappoint you*
Load Javascript in Footer:	☑ *(Recommended, else loaded in header)*
Disable on Mobile Device:	☑ *(Disable on iPad,iPhone,Blackberry,Nokia,Opera Mini and Android)*

I recommend you uncheck the border (which draws a box around the buttons) and remove the check next to **Show Background Color**. Your buttons will then look more integrated into your site's pages.

The disable on mobile devices is checked by default. That is probably because they found some problems displaying these on mobile devices. Therefore, I'd leave that unchecked for now, but try it later on when you have a change to view your site on an iPad, Android tablet and Smartphones.

Next, if you have a Twitter ID, add it without the @ symbol.

Your Twitter ID: ezSEONews| *Specify your twitter id without @*

The next set of options is only valid if you chose to display the buttons on the left side (when you chose the position of the buttons).

Left Side Floating Specific Options

Left Side Spacing: 60px *Spacing from Left Side of Margin*

Top Spacing: 40% *Spacing from Top of the page*

Float Bar Position: Fixed Position ▼

If you are displaying the buttons on the left side, you can play with these floating options to make sure they look OK on your site.

The final settings are for width and count display.

You can leave these at their default values and only come back to change things if you find a problem with how the buttons look on your pages.

OK, click the **Save Changes** button and then go visit your website.

Demo Post

ddsf adsf da fsd f sdf asdf asdf asdf sdaf asdf ddsf adsf da fsd f sdf asdf asdf
asdf ddsf adsf da fsd f sdf asdf asdf asdf sdaf asdf ddsf adsf da fsd f sdf asdf
sdaf asdf ddsf adsf da fsd f sdf asdf asdf asdf sdaf asdf ddsf adsf da fsd f sdf

Other social share plugins

Over the years I have tried lots of social sharing plugins. Some work great, while others only seem to work on some websites and not others. If you find the plugin above does not work properly on *your* site, just search for "social share" in the Add Plugins screen, and try some.

Tasks to complete

    1. Install the social sharing plugin and set it up to suit your needs.

Differences with pages

As we discussed earlier, pages are different to posts. On the Add/Edit Page screen, it all looks very similar, but there are a few notable omissions - namely no categories or tags! There is also no box to add an excerpt. These are no great loss to us, as we don't use pages for important articles/content on the site.

We do, however, have a couple of options for pages that are not found in posts - Page Attributes:

```
Page Attributes

Parent

(no parent)          ▼

Template

Default Template     ▼

Order

0

Need help? Use the Help tab in the upper right
of your screen.
```

Since we are only using pages for our "legal" content (and "About" page), these new settings don't really apply to our site. However, you might be interested, so I'll explain what they are.

The page attributes allow you to do the following: Set up parent-child relationships between your pages, choose a template for your page, and set the order of your pages. Let's look at what this means to you.

A Parent Child relationship between pages is similar to the relationship we saw earlier with categories. Any page can have a parent page, and the level of parent-child relationships can be many levels deep.

For example, you might have a page called Disclaimers.

You might then set up other pages on your site called Medical Disclaimer, Outbound link Disclaimer, Affiliate Disclaimer and so on. For each of these pages you make the **Disclaimers** page the parent. We therefore have this type of relationship:

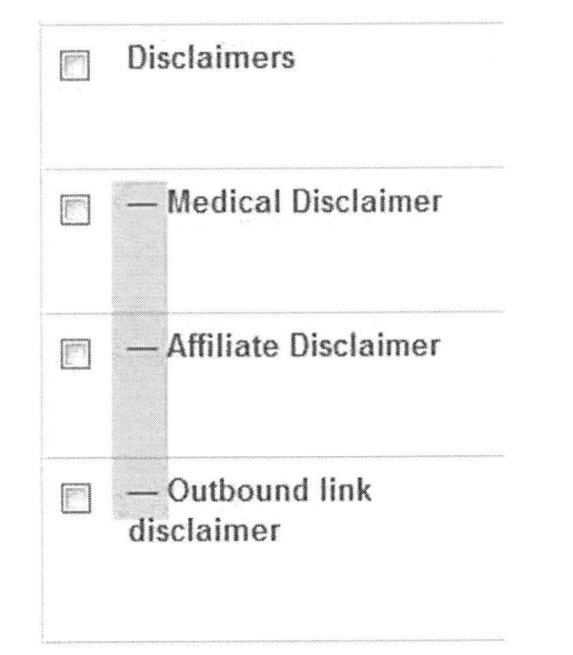

With WordPress templates, like the Twenty Eleven template we are using here, it recognizes and handles this type of parent-child page relationship, so when adding these pages to the navigation bar, you get this dropdown menu:

The child disclaimers are listed underneath the parent page. This saves space on the navigation menu.

The biggest problem with parent child pages is that not all themes support them. Because of this I don't bother using parent child pages. Instead, if I want to create the type of hierarchy seen in the menu above, I will create a custom menu, which we'll look at a little later on in the book.

The next Page Attribute is the Template.

Template

Showcase Template ▾

| Default Template |
| **Showcase Template** |
| Sidebar Template |

The templates you have available for your pages depend on the theme you are using. Some themes don't have any additional page templates, while others may have several. As you can see, the Twenty Eleven template comes with a total of three templates to choose from.

The **Default Template:** Shows main content but no sidebar.

The **Sidebar template:** Shows the main content with a sidebar.

The **Showcase template:** I'll leave that for you to find out.

For any theme you use, you'll need to read the documentation (or experiment yourself), with the page templates to see what they each do.

The final Page Attribute is the order. This is where you can supply a numerical value to order your pages (number 1 being the first page). This is only useful when you leave the responsibility of creating navigation bars to WordPress. If you haven't set the order, then WordPress uses its own default values for deciding which page should be listed first.

We won't be setting the page order for our "legal pages" because we will create custom menus later. These custom menus will show our pages EXACTLY as we want them, without the hassles of setting up parent-child pages or changing the order.

Tasks to complete

1. Go and look at the Page Edit screen. Note the page attributes box. Have a look at the settings by pulling down the drop down box to show the page templates.

2. Set up a parent page and two or three child pages. There doesn't have to be any content on them. Once done, check out the menu on your site to see how WordPress handles parent-child pages.

Internal linking of posts

One of the best ways of keeping visitors on your site is to interlink the content on your pages. There are a few ways of doing this.

The basic way is to manually add links from one page to another. This is easily done in the WYSIWYG editor.

Just highlight a word or phrase that you want to link to another post on the site:

.. and then click the link button in the toolbar. A popup box will appear asking for details of where and how you want to link to that other page:

The very top box is asking for the URL of the webpage you want to link to. I recommend you ALWAYS begin this with http:// or your links to other sites won't work.

If you know the URL of the webpage, that's fine. Just paste it in. I usually open the webpage in a separate tab of my browser and copy the URL from the address bar to paste into the URL box.

If you are linking to a webpage on your own site, there is a link labeled **Or link to existing content**, which if you click, opens a box at the bottom that lists all of the content on your site. There is a search box there to help you find stuff more easily. Once you see the page you want to link to in this list, just click it. The URL and title will be filled in for you by WordPress.

WARNING: I recommend that with all internal linking on your site you leave the title attribute BLANK. The reason is simply that Google are on the warpath. They are penalizing websites that appear to be over-optimized and the link's title attribute has been one place that spammers have abused in the past. Adding in any kind of keyword rich title could eventually cause your site problems. So be safe, and leave the link's title tag empty.

Your final choice for the link is whether to open it in a new window or not. I have a general rule of thumb with this option. If I am linking to another page on my own site, I open it in the same window (so leave that checkbox empty). If I am linking to a page on another website (and may therefore lose the visitor from my own site), then I'll have the link open in a new window/tab, by checking that box.

With all the settings filled in, click the Add link button to add the link to your article.

OK, that's the 100% manual way of inter-linking your content.

One way I recommend you inter-link your content is with a plugin called **Yet Another Related Posts** plugin. This plugin allows you to set up a "Related Articles" section at the end of your posts. This will automatically link to articles that the plugin deems related (according to parameters you set up).

Go to the **Add New** Plugin screen and search for **yet another related post**.

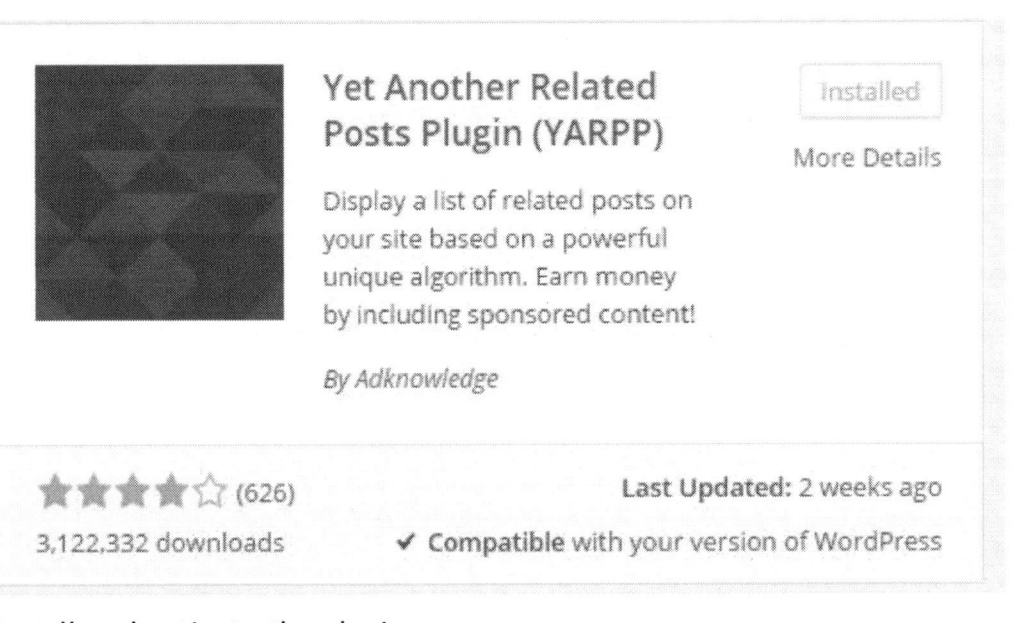

Install and activate the plugin.

You will now find the YARPP settings inside the main settings menu:

Click on the link to the settings so we can set this up.

The first thing to do when you get to the YARPP settings page is open up the Screen Options at the top:

Show on screen

☑ "The Pool" ☑ "Relatedness" options ☑ Display options for your website

☑ Display options for RSS ☑ Help Improve YARPP ☑ Contact YARPP

☐ Show example code output

Screen Options ▲

Yet Another Related Posts Plugin Options
4.0.6

Check **"The Pool"** and **"Relatedness"** options.

The pool is something you might want to switch off at some point. I don't use it, but I always suggest turning everything on until you get an idea of what a thing does. At that point you can decide whether to turn them off or not.

OK, let's set up the plugin.

So the top options on the page are the "Pool":

"The Pool"

"The Pool" refers to the pool of posts and pages that are candidates for display as related to the current entry.

Post types considered: Posts, Pages more>

Disallow by Category: ☐ Brakes ☐ Engine ☐ Exhaust ☐ Toyota ☐ Wordpress Tutorials

Disallow by Tag: ☐ new post ☐ test

☐ Show password protected posts?

☐ Show only posts from the past   12   month(s) ▼

You can leave these options set at their defaults. The Pool does give you some power over what posts are shown in the related posts section of your articles. You can decide not to allow posts to be included based on category or tag. You can also show password protected posts or only posts from the last X number of months, weeks or days.

Since I leave everything at the default level, I turn this off in the screen options.

Next up are the relatedness options.

"Relatedness" options

YARPP limits the related posts list by (1) a maximum number and (2) a *match threshold*. more>

Match threshold: 5

Titles: consider

Bodies: consider

Categories: consider

Tags: consider

☐ Display results from all post types more>

☐ Show only previous posts?

Again, for now you can leave these options set at their default values. The only thing you might like to play with is decreasing the **Match Threshold** if you are getting a "No related posts found" message at the end of your posts. I'd consider reducing this to a 4, then a 3, then a 2, then a 1.5 and so on, until the related posts are (1) shown, and (2) related to the post/article they appear on. This is something you can only really do when you have a number of posts on your site.

For now, leave everything as it is and when you have more content, check out the related post section after each post and play with the threshold until you're happy.

Next up are the Display options. These basically tell the plugin how you want your posts displayed in the related posts section.

Display options for your website

Automatically display: ⑦   ☑ Posts   ☐ Pages   ☐ Media

☐ Also display in archives

Maximum number of related posts: 4

| List | Thumbnails | <?php Custom |

Before / after related entries: `<h3>Related pos` / `</ol>`   *For example: <ol>*

Before / after each related entry: `<li>` / `</li>`   *For example: <li><*

☑ Show excerpt?

Excerpt length (No. of words):   10

Before / after (excerpt):   `<small>` / `</small>`   *For example: <li></li> or <dl></dl*

Default display if no results: `<p>No related posts.</p>`

Order results: score (high relevance to low) ▾

☐ Help promote Yet Another Related Posts Plugin? ⑦

At the top, make sure **Automatically display** in posts is checked. You might like to uncheck this if you decide later to include related posts in the sidebar instead of at the end of each post. Wait until we cover widgets before you decide.

Next you can choose the maximum number of related posts to show. The default is 4, but you might like to reduce this to 3.

Check the box labeled **Show Excerpts?** (this will show the post description with a link).

That's it for this section of settings.

The last option in these settings is to display related posts in feeds.

Display options for RSS

☐ Display related posts in feeds? ❓

Leave this UNCHECKED.

Now save the changes.

NOTE: You can create your own templates for formatting related posts using this plugin. Since this requires some PHP knowledge, we won't be covering it in this book. However, if you are interested in exploring more options for the display of your related posts section, look at the help documents of this plugin. You will find links to the YARPP website & forum in the top right of the settings screen.

Here is an example of a related posts section on one of my sites using this plugin.

Related Posts

1. Can Citrus Fruit Juice Help Clear Up Acne?
   Vitamin C is a powerful anti-inflammatory that can help take the anger out oof spots and pimples. Citrus juicing is therefore a good way to help reduce inflammation caused by acne.

2. Serrapeptase and Nattokinase enzymes may help clear up Acne
   Enzymes such as serropeptase and nattokinase (two naturally occuring enzymes) can help to clear up acne. In this article we'll look at how staph bacteria cause acne, and how the ezymes can help.

3. Weight Loss & Acne – How Juicing Can Help With Both Problems
   Adolescents often have two "nightmares" at the same time. Weight and acne! In this article, we'll look at how juicing can help with both.

4. Can Probiotics Help with your Acne Problem?
   Probiotics are helpful bacteria found in yoghurt that live in our intestines and help break up fiber and recycle hormones as well as create vitamin K. They are also important in the control of acne.

This related posts section was on a post about acne. Can you see the benefits? People who are reading the main acne article are shown other articles related to the condition. It gives us another chance to keep the visitor on our site.

We have looked at two ways we can inter-link our content. Firstly we can manually create links within the content. Secondly we can use a plugin like YARPP to show related posts to our visitors.

The last option I like to use is a plugin that I can set up to control internal linking on a much more automated basis, and without losing control over the linking.

I have written an article on internal site linking using this plugin. If you are interested, you should read that article here:

http://ezseonews.com/backlinks/internal-linking-seo/

Tasks to complete

1. Install YARPP and configure it.

2. Go and edit an existing post, or create one for this exercise and add links manually to a couple of other pages on your site (or on another website altogether).

3. Open the page in a web browser and check that the links you added work properly.

Homepage of your site - blog or static?

WordPress is a tool that was created initially for blogs. That is, websites that publish date-related content as posts. The way in which WordPress handles these posts by default is to post them on the homepage, with the latest post at the top of that page. In the settings, we saw that we could define how many posts to include on a page with the default set at 10. That means the last 10 posts published on the site will show up on the homepage in chronological order, with the latest post at the top and older posts below. As you post more content to the site, the older posts scroll off the bottom of the homepage and are replaced by the newer ones at the top.

If that is the type of site you want, then that's fine. You can ignore this section and leave things at their default settings.

Personally, I like to create a homepage where I have more control over the content being displayed. I like to create the homepage so that it always displays my "homepage article". The homepage article is there to help visitors find their way around my site. This type of organisation is typical of non-WordPress sites. The good news is that it's easy to do in WordPress. You just need to write the "homepage article" as a PAGE, not a POST.

Once you have created that article, go to the Reading Settings inside the main settings menu of the Dashboard Navigation.

At the top of the screen there are two radio buttons with **Your latest posts** selected as default. You need to select the **A static page** option.

Now two drop down boxes will appear. The top one labelled **Front Page** is the one we are interested in. Simply click on the drop down box and select the page you created with your homepage article.

At the bottom of your page, click on the Save Changes button.

OK you are all set. Go to your homepage and you'll see the main article being displayed. No matter how many posts you add to your site, that homepage will not change (unless you change it).

OK, I hear your question.

"If the homepage just shows the same article, how are people going to find all my other content on the website?"

Well, that's where the sidebar, widgets and custom menus come in. We'll look at those next.

NOTE: If you have completed this exercise to turn a page into your homepage and you are not seeing the sidebar on the homepage, go in and edit the page and change the page temple to one that uses a sidebar. On the Twenty Eleven theme, that option is **Sidebar Template**.

That will force the homepage PAGE to use a template with a sidebar, which we'll need in the next section.

Incidentally, if your site is showing a comment form on the homepage and you want to turn this off, just go in and edit the page again. There is a section there called Discussion (if you don't see it, check the screen options at the top).

Simply uncheck the option to **Allow comments** (and trackbacks and pingbacks if you wish), and then re-publish the page by clicking the update button.

Tasks to complete

1. If you want your homepage to show the same article, create a PAGE with that article, and then go and edit the Settings -> Reading so that the page you created is static on the front page.

Widgets

Widgets are basically plugins that allow you to easily add visual and interactive components to your site without needing any technical knowledge.

If you want to add a list of recent posts, you can do it easily by using a widget. Perhaps you want to add a poll to your site? Well, that can be done with widgets too.

When a designer creates a WordPress theme, their initial drawing will probably have "widgitized" blocks drawn onto it, so that they can visualize which areas will accept widgets. Maybe it will look something like this example (with the red/shaded areas able to accept the widgets):

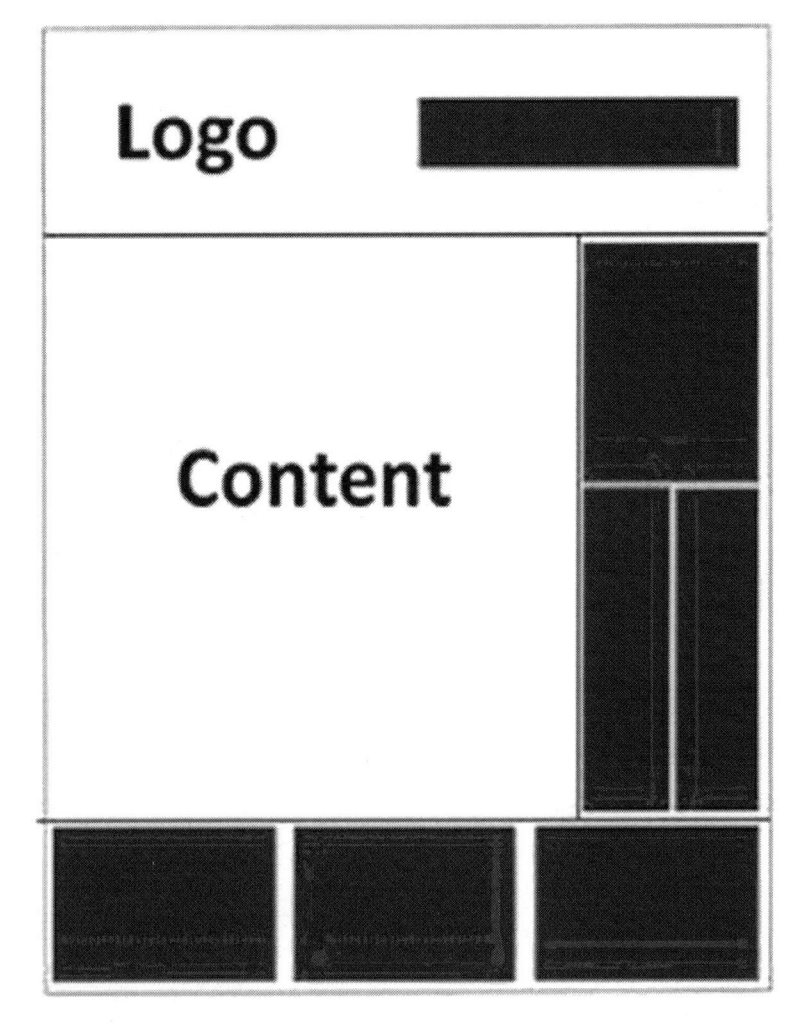

The usual areas that accept widgets are sidebars and footers. However, some themes have extensive widget capabilities, with even the entire homepage being widgetized.

We'll have a look at the standard widgets that come with WordPress in a moment, but first, let's see which areas of the Twenty Eleven theme can take widgets.

Login to your Dashboard and go to the Appearance -> Widgets menu.

This will take you to an area where you can set up the widgets on your website. On the right you'll see some collapsible rectangles that represent the areas on the site that can accept widgets. As I have mentioned before, this will be different for each template, but for the Twenty Eleven theme, this is what we've got to work with:

Main Sidebar

    Meta

Showcase Sidebar

Footer Area One

Footer Area Two

Footer Area Three

There are 5 areas of the website that can accept widgets.

The Main Sidebar: That's the sidebar that appears on your homepage, all of your posts and whichever pages use the sidebar template. You'll notice that there is

197

already a widget in that area of my site. It's called Meta, and that adds some links to the main sidebar that you can see below:

If you remember, when we were clearing out the pre-installed widgets, I left that one in there so I could have a quick-link to login to my website. If I wanted to remove those links from my site, I'd simply delete that widget.

There is also an area called Showcase Sidebar, which can accept widgets. This is the sidebar that is shown on pages (not posts), that use the Showcase page template. If you want to experiment with the showcase page, do so (the sidebar may not appear where you expect it to).

The other three widgetized areas on the Twenty Eleven theme are the three footer areas, which represent the left, middle and right positions.

Let's add a simply text widget to each of these areas so we can see the effects on our site. A text widget is a widget that will display text (or HTML), in a widgetized area of your website.

Let's do it together so you can get a feel for how to use these widgets.

Click on the little arrowhead pointing down in the top right hand corner of the **Footer Area One** widgets area. This will open it up.

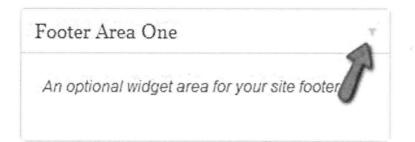

Now click and drag a text widget from the **Available widgets**, and drop it (by releasing the mouse button), in the Footer Area One.

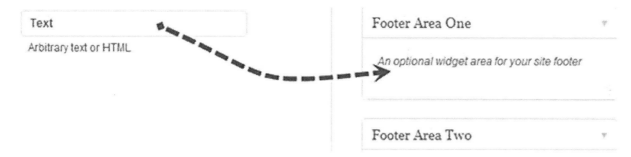

The text widget will open up for editing its settings.

Footer Area One ▼

An optional widget area for your site footer

Text ▼

Title:

_____

[large empty text box]

☐ Automatically add paragraphs

Delete | Close   ◎ **Save**

At the top of the text widget you can enter a title. Enter Text Widget 1.

In the big box underneath (which would normally hold the text or html code you wanted to insert into your page), enter the same thing – Text Widget 1.

When done, click the Save button, on the bottom right side, to save your widget settings.

Repeat for Footer Area Two and Three, but change the text widget title and text to Text Widget 2 and Text Widget 3 respectively.

Now go and view your website. Scroll down to the footer area:

TEXT WIDGET 1	TEXT WIDGET 2	TEXT WIDGET 3
Text Widget 1	Text Widget 2	Text Widget 3

Proudly powered by WordPress

You can see that the three widgets you added appear in the bottom left, middle, and right positions of the footer. These areas correspond to the three widgetized areas. Cool eh? Using the text widget you can add any text or HTML to these areas of your website.

When playing around to see what widgets do and how they appear on your site, I recommend filling in all of the settings for the widget. In this example we entered a title and the main text. We can see how the WordPress template handles the formatting of the title and the text. The title is all uppercase and the main text is normal.

Let's have a look at the standard widgets that are already installed.

Available Widgets

Drag widgets from here to a sidebar on the right to activate them. Drag widgets back here to deactivate them and delete their settings.

Archives

A monthly archive of your site's posts

Calendar

A calendar of your site's posts

Categories

A list or dropdown of categories

Custom Menu

Use this widget to add one of your custom menus as a widget.

Meta

Log in/out, admin, feed and WordPress links

Pages

Your site's WordPress Pages

Recent Comments

The most recent comments

Recent Posts

The most recent posts on your site

Related Posts (YARPP)

Related Posts (YARPP)

RSS

Entries from any RSS or Atom feed

Search

A search form for your site

Tag Cloud

Your most used tags in cloud format

Text

Arbitrary text or HTML

Twenty Eleven Ephemera

Use this widget to list your recent Aside, Status, Quote, and Link posts

I am not going to go through these, as they are fairly self-explanatory. Besides, you can always add them yourself and see what they do, and remove them just as easily if need be.

Hopefully you can now see the potential of widgets.

You are not just limited to the widgets that come pre-installed with WordPress. Many plugins or services provide their own WordPress widget so that you can add new features to your website as you build it up. For example, you'll notice that there is a YARPP widget that was installed with the Yet Another Related Posts plugin. That widget will add a list of related posts to your sidebar in case you don't want them displayed after the post (which we enabled in the settings previously by choosing to automatically show related posts after the article).

Basic HTML

One thing that will come in handy is some simple HTML code that you might like to use in widgets. You can add HTML to a text widget. For example, if you want to add some text with a link to another page, you'd just look up the HTML below for creating a hyperlink and insert it into your text widget accordingly.

A hyperlink

<a href="URL">LINK TEXT</a>

Just replace URL with the web address of the page you want to link to, and the LINK TEXT with the word or phrase you want linked.

Example:

If you are interested, you can read my review of the <a href="http://blenderreview.com/waring">waring blender</a> for more details.

It I entered that into a sidebar text widget, it would look like this on my site:

META

- Site Admin
- Log out
- Entries RSS
- Comments RSS
- WordPress.org

EXAMPLE LINK

If you are interested, you can read my review of the waring blender for more details.

I added a title to the text widget (Example link). You can see the phrase "waring blender" is a link to the URL I specified in the HTML.

An image

To insert an image, here is the HTML:

<img src="URL" width="XX" height="YY" />

Replace URL with the URL of the image (upload it via the media library and grab the URL there), XX is the width in pixels and YY is the height in pixels. If your image is the correct size (which it should be to keep image load times to a minimum), then you can leave out the height and width parameters and the code just becomes:

<img src="URL" />

For example, using an image from my media library, I grabbed the URL for the image and inserted it into a text widget. This is what it looks like:

META

- Site Admin
- Log out
- Entries RSS
- Comments RSS
- WordPress.org

EXAMPLE IMAGE

A numbered list

The HTML for a numbered list is a little more complicated.

```
<ol>
  <li>item one</li>
  <li>item two</li>
  <li>item three</li>
</ol>
```

You simply replace item one, item two, item three and so on with whatever you want displayed. You can add as many items as you need. Just repeat the <li>item</li> code once for each item you want to add.

For example, here is some code which shows a numbered list for my top three tablet recommendations.

```
<ol>
  <li>Asus 301</li>
  <li>Asus 201</li>
  <li>Apple iPad</li>
</ol>
```

.. and this is what it looks like in a sidebar text widget.

META

- Site Admin
- Log out
- Entries RSS
- Comments RSS
- WordPress.org

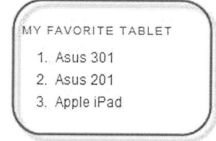

MY FAVORITE TABLET

1. Asus 301
2. Asus 201
3. Apple iPad

NOTE: The text you add for an item CAN be a hyperlink. Just construct it from the HTML I showed you above.

A bullet list

A bulleted list is almost the same code as the numbered list with one modification.

Instead of the code opening with <ol> and closing with </ol>, a bullet list opens with <ul> and closes with </ul>. The "ol" stands for ordered list (ordered by number), whereas the "ul" stands for unordered list.

```
<ul>
  <li>item one</li>
  <li>item two</li>
  <li>item three</li>
</ul>
```

Here is my widget now:

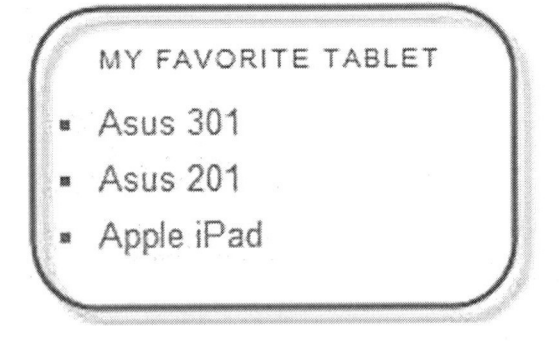

That should give you enough HTML to get you started with text widgets.

There is one other widget that I do want to discuss in a little more detail. It goes hand-in-hand with one of the features we haven't looked at yet, which are custom menus. The widget itself is used to display a custom menu in a widgetized area. We therefore need a custom menu first, so that's where we'll begin

Tasks to complete

1. Go and explore the widgets area. Add some widgets to your site and then view the site in your browser to see what they do and how they format the information.

2. Add in a text widget and experiment with the HTML code I gave you in this chapter. Try adding a text widget to the top of the sidebar with a photograph of yourself (or your persona image), and a brief bio.

Custom menus

To add or edit a custom menu in WordPress, go to the **Menus** item inside the **Appearance** menu:

If you have been following along as you've read this book, you will have noticed that every time you created a new page, WordPress added it to the menu on your site.

NOTE: When the WP policies plugin created a lot of pages for us, these were not added to the menu. Pages only get added to the menu when we actually go in and create the page manually.

Here is the menu that WordPress has built for me:

Learning Wo

Home   Contact   Disclaimers

Medical Disclaimer

Affiliate Disclaimer

My Homep   Outbound link disclaimer

fgsfdg sfdg fds gsfd gdsf g fdsg dfsg dfs gsfd gfd gfgsfdg sfdg fds gsfd gdsf g fdsg
dfs gsfd gfd gfgsfdg sfdg fds gsfd gdsf g fdsg dfsg dfs gsfd gfd gfgsfdg sfdg fds gs

This is not how I want my navigation menu to appear. The good thing is I don't have to put up with it, because I can create my own custom menu.

Let's now design a custom menu to replace the one above.

In the custom menu screen, the first thing you need to do is click the **create a new menu** link.

Type in a name for your menu (I've called mine "Top Menu"), and then click the **Create Menu** button.

When the page refreshes, immediately click the **Save Menu** button.

At the top of the screen you'll see a tab labeled **Manage Locations**.

Click it.

This screen tells us how many custom menus our theme supports. The Twenty Eleven theme supports only one - the **Primary menu.**

That is the menu we want to replace.

NOTE: This limit on the number of custom menus supported does not affect your ability to put custom menus in the sidebar, as that is controlled by a plugin, not the theme.

OK, from the drop down menu labelled **Primary Menu**, select the menu you just created and then click Save. That tells WordPress we want to use our own menu and not the one WordPress created for us automatically.

Since our custom menu is presently empty, if we now check our site, the old menu has gone. Go and visit your homepage to check. The menu should no longer be there. If it's still visible, make sure you have saved the menu AND saved the menu selection for the Primary location.

OK, time to build our new menu.

Building a menu is easy. For the most part, you can select from the lists that WordPress gives us on this screen. However, for the first link in my menu, I want a link called "Home" that links back to my homepage. To add this, we need to add a **custom link**. A custom link is just one we need to build ourselves as opposed to selecting it from the list that WordPress presents us with.

On the left you'll see a box labelled **Links**.

Just enter your homepage URL (making sure to include the http://), in the URL box. Next, add the text you want displayed for that menu item in the Label box. And finally, click the **Add to Menu** button.

| Menu Name | Top Menu | Save Menu |

Menu Structure

Drag each item into the order you prefer. Click the arrow on the right of the item to reveal additional configuration options.

| Home | Custom ▼ |

Menu Settings

Auto add pages ☐ Automatically add new top-level pages to this menu

Theme locations ☐ Primary Menu

Delete Menu   Save Menu

A box now appears in the menu we are building on the right.

Notice that the box has an arrowhead on the right side labelled **Custom**. The box is currently collapsed, but it can be expanded with that arrowhead where we can access to some of the settings:

Yours will have fewer settings in it than mine because some are hidden by default. To see all of the settings that are visible in my screenshot, simply check the boxes in the **Screen Options** (top right). The only box in the screen options that I would leave unchecked is the **Format** box. You can uncheck others later, once you know what they do and whether or not you need them.

The main settings for each link are as follows:

• **URL** – the URL (web address), that you are linking to.

• **Navigation Label** – the text that is displayed for the link.

• **Title Attribute** – Do NOT use this; leave it blank. Remember we mentioned earlier about getting into trouble with Google for stuffing keywords into a link's "title" attribute?

• **Open link in a new Window/tab** – useful if you are linking to another website, but all links to pages on your own site should have this option unchecked.

• **CSS Classes** – don't worry about this. It's an advanced feature for people who want more control over the way the menu links look.

• **Link Relationship (XFN)** – this can actually be useful on occasions if you want to set the "nofollow" attribute on a link. I set links to all "legal" pages as "nofollow", and this is the box where I do that. We'll see it in a minute as I continue to construct my menu.

NOTE: Nofollow simply tells the search engines not to follow the link. It's a good idea to nofollow links to sites you don't really trust.

• **Description** – is sometimes displayed by the theme, but not all themes support this attribute. I would therefore ignore this feature and even uncheck it in the screen options.

OK, with the home link in my menu, my site now has a functioning custom menu:

There is only one link in the menu, but it's a start. Let's add some more.

As we move down the options on the left (underneath the **Custom Links**), is the **Posts** section:

Posts ▲

Most Recent | View All | Search

☐ My Books

Select All | Add to Menu

This section lists the most recent posts on your site, though there are tabs to view *all* posts and even search for posts. If you want to add a link to a particular post in your menu, select the check box next to that post and click the **Add to Menu** button. The post will then appear in the menu. I don't want any POSTS in my menu at the moment, but I do want some PAGES. That's the next section down:

Pages

Most Recent   View All   Search

- ☐ Testimonial Disclaimer
- ☐ Terms Of Use
- ☐ Privacy Policy
- ☐ Medical Disclaimer
- ☐ External Links Policy
- ☐ Earnings Disclaimer
- ☐ E-mail Policy
- ☐ Dmca Notice

Select All   Add to Menu

Just select the pages you want included in your navigation menu and then click the **Add to Menu** button.

The pages will now appear in the list on the right. There are three other types of links we can add to our custom menu; the most useful being Categories and Tags:

Categories ▲

Most Used   View All   Search

☐ My Books

Select All   Add to Menu

Tags ▼

Format ▼

These options allow you to add links in your menus to category pages and tag pages.

If there are important category or tag pages on your site, it might be something you want to add to your own menu (or maybe a custom menu in the sidebar using a custom menu widget!)

OK, I have now added all of the links I want in my menu bar, but there's a problem; on the site, it's looking kind of messy!

My Homepage Article

META

- Site Adm
- Log out

I would like to have my menu bar display in this order: Home first, WordPress Tutorials next, then Contact, and finally a hierarchical menu that lists all of the disclaimers and "legal" pages. OK, so let's re-organise the menu items.

The Custom Menu Designer has the drag and drop feature. This means you can click and hold down your mouse button to pick up a menu item, drag it to the place you want it located, and then unclick your mouse button to drop it there. That is the simple procedure of how we can re-order the items in our menu in just a few seconds.

After dragging my menu items into the order I want them to appear, this is what I now have:

Home	Custom ▼
Wordpress Tutorials	Category ▼
Contact	Page ▼
Disclaimers	Page ▼
Terms Of Use	Page ▼
Privacy Policy	Page ▼
External Links Policy	Page ▼

The only snag now is getting those legal pages into a hierarchy, with the last three items appearing as a drop down menu of the Disclaimers menu. But don't worry, that's easy too.

To create a "child menu", drag the menu item to the right a little, just underneath the item you want as its parent (see below):

Home	Custom ▾

Wordpress Tutorials	Category ▾

Contact	Page ▾

Disclaimers	Page ▾

Terms Of Use	Page ▾

Privacy Policy	Page ▾

External Links Policy	Page ▾

Do you see how the Terms of Use, Privacy Policy and External Links Policy are all lined up and indented under the Disclaimers menu item? That makes them child menus of the Disclaimers menu. So on my site now, the menu system looks like this (after saving everything of course).

Do you see how powerful the custom menu designer is?

We don't have to rely on WordPress to create the site navigation. We can easily create a navigation menu system without the fuss of using parent/child pages and setting page order. If you design your own navigation menu, you get more flexible menus. In other words, menus that display exactly as YOU want them to.

OK, so one final thing. Any custom menu you create can be added to a sidebar using the custom menu widget. I'm just going to create another menu quickly so I can show you how this works.

First, I need to add a new menu:

.. add a name, and click **Create Menu**.

I'll just add a couple of posts to the menu using the Posts selector and then save my new menu.

OK, now it's time to head back to the Appearance -> Widgets screen.

When you get there, drag a custom menu widget into the Main Sidebar:

You can add a title for the widget and select the menu you want displayed. Save the widget, then check out the sidebar on your homepage. Here is mine:

META

- Site Admin
- Log out
- Entries RSS
- Comments RSS
- WordPress.org

MY FAVORITE TABLET

- Asus 301
- Asus 201
- Apple iPad

FAVORITE POSTS

- Demo Post
- Hello world!

You can create custom menus for all kinds of things. These may be top review pages or important tag pages. The point is this; custom menus give you the flexibility you need as you design and develop your website.

Tasks to complete

1. Go and experiment with Custom Menus.

2. Create a menu with a "Home" link and links to the "legal" pages on your site. Don't worry if you're unsure about what you want to add to the menu(s), as you can always update things later. And of course, any changes will be effective immediately, the moment you hit the Save button.

Viewing your site while logged in

Something special happens when you are visiting your website while logged into your Dashboard.

Earlier, when we were looking at the User Profile, we made sure an option was checked – **Show Toolbar when viewing site.** Let's have a look what happens with that option enabled.

Login to your dashboard and then open your website in another tab of your web browser.

What you'll see is a very useful "ribbon" across the top of your website:

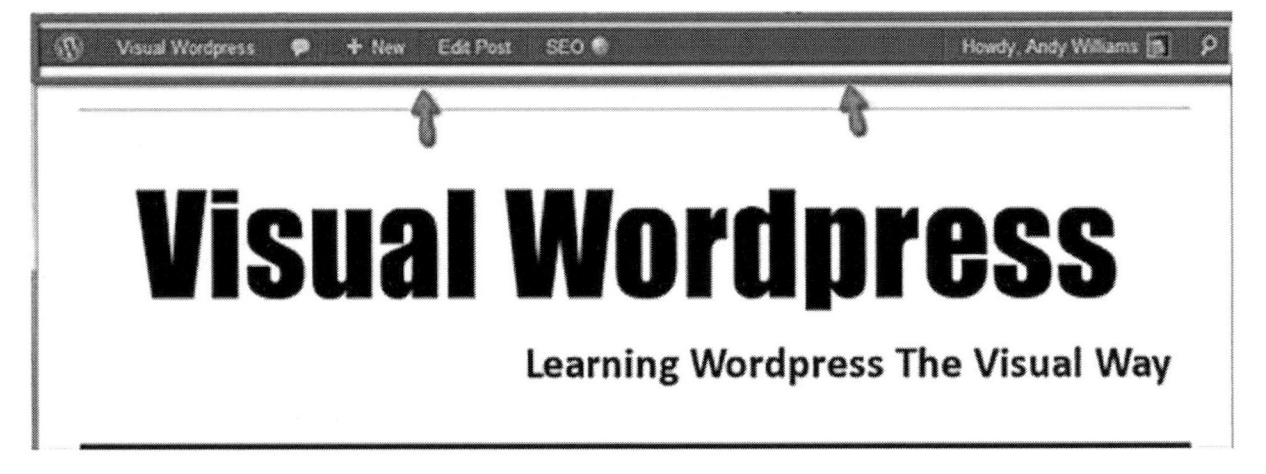

This ribbon gives you access to some important WordPress features. For example, if you want to edit a page or post on your website, you can visit your website, find the post, then click on the edit post link in the ribbon bar (you can see it in the screenshot above). That link will open up the post in the WordPress Dashboard ready for editing.

The ribbon is very useful as you browse your site. If you find errors, just click the **Edit Post** link, fix the issue(s), and then click the Update button.

The other main features of the ribbon are the two drop down menus:

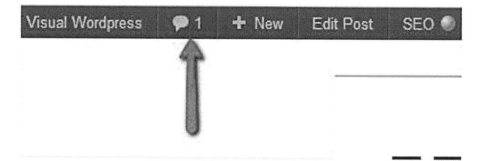

The first one gives you access to your Dashboard, Themes, Customize, Widgets, Menus, Background and Header settings.

The other menu allows you to add a new Posts or Page, access Media, add a Link, or open the new User setup page. Now some of these features won't be much use, but it is nice having them there in case you need them at any time.

The biggest benefit of this ribbon, to me, is the Edit Post link AND the speech bubble.

See that number one next to the speech bubble? That means there is a comment awaiting moderation. Clicking the speech bubble will open up the Dashboard at the moderate comments screen.

Tasks to complete

1. Login to your site.
2. Open the site in a new tab in your browser.
3. Explore the ribbon bar at the top and see what quick options are accessible from it.

WordPress security

WordPress has often been criticized as being too easy to hack. There have been a lot of cases where people have lost their WordPress site after a hacker gained access to it and wreaked havoc. Several years ago, one of my sites got hacked so badly that I just deleted the whole thing and let the domain expire. At that time, I didn't have a reliable backup system in place. It is therefore wise to take the security of your site very seriously.

Earlier in the book we set up a plugin which is sending us database backups every week or so via email. That's a great start, but the plugin does not backup everything we need to restore a site. It doesn't backup the theme, plugins, or any customizations we may have made.

To create a complete backup of my sites, I use a script that I bought called WP Twin. This script creates a perfect backup of a website (which includes things like theme settings and plugins). If a site of mine ever did get hacked again, I could restore the entire project with a few simple clicks of the mouse (or even move the site to an entirely different domain).

WP Twin is a premium script that isn't cheap. Knowing that most people have a tight budget when starting out, I had a look around for a free alternative. I found one that has good reviews, but have not used it myself. It's called Duplicator and you install it the same way you do for any plugin. Just search for Duplicator in the add plugins screen of your dashboard.

Duplicator

Duplicate, clone, backup, move and transfer an entire site from one location to another.

By LifeInTheGrid

Install Now

More Details

★★★★★ (734)

821,462 downloads

Last Updated: 3 weeks ago

✔ **Compatible** with your version of WordPress

Disclaimer: I have not used this plugin so cannot show you how it works or personally vouch for it in any way.

What this plugin will allow you to do is take an exact snapshot of your site and all its data, which would then allow a complete reconstruction of the site if anything bad happened. I would keep the database backups coming via email as well, but Duplicator will provide you with another layer of cover should you ever need it.

Another layer of protection is to **always upgrade WordPress** as soon as there is a new update available.

The WordPress team fix security leaks as soon as they are found. Therefore, if your Dashboard says there is a WordPress upgrade; install it as soon as possible to make sure your copy of the software is up-to-date with any bug fixes and or new security patches.

Finally, I also use a script on all of my sites that helps protect against hackers. It is a commercial script, but it is cheap. I have used the script (on over 100 websites), ever since I lost that site to hackers. I haven't had any problems with hackers since. The script is called WP-Secure and you can read about it here:

http://ezseonews.com/secure-wordpress/

Tasks to complete

1. Always keep WordPress up to date.
2. Install a backup plugin, like Duplicator, and make a full backup of your site.
3. Consider getting the WP-Secure plugin and installing it to prevent hackers from gaining access to your site.

Monitoring website traffic

Every Webmaster wants to know how many visitors their site is getting and how those people are finding their pages (through search engines, via social media channels, etc.).

Fortunately there are a number of good, free solutions to give you this information.

The tool I use on my own sites is called Google Analytics, but it is complex and perhaps overkill for someone just starting out. I'd therefore recommend you use a free service like Get Clicky - http://clicky.com/

Head on over there now and sign up for an account.

The signup process is just a simple form that asks for your email, real name, username, and password. Then of course it asks which domain you want to track. Just enter the full URL of your website.

After signing up, you'll be logged into your account preferences. You don't need to do anything in there (unless you want to). For now, just click through to your Dashboard:

When you get there it will look a little empty:

It will remain empty too, at least until you add some tracking code to your website so that Get Clicky can monitor visitors on your site.

To add this code to your site, I recommend another plugin by the same guy that created the WordPress SEO plugin. This one is called "Clicky by Yoast".

Go to your Dashboard Plugins area and click on **Add New**. Then search for **Clicky by Yoast**.

Clicky by Yoast

Integrates the Clicky web analytics service into your blog and adds features for comment tracking & more.

By Team Yoast

Install Now

More Details

★★★★☆ (70)

212,709 downloads

Last Updated: 3 months ago

Untested with your version of WordPress

Install and activate the plugin.

You'll find the settings for the plugin inside the main Setting menu of the Dashboard Navigation:

We need set up the plugin so that our website can communicate with Get Clicky. Click on **Clicky** in settings menu to open up the options for this plugin.

Open the Get Clicky website in another tab of your browser and login.

You should have the Clicky settings in your WordPress Dashboard open in one tab, and your Get Clicky account opened in a second tab.

Click on the **Preferences** link over at Get Clicky:

230

Goals Spy Big screen Twitter Alerts Preferences

Visitors

— Yesterday   — Today

You'll see information about your site that you'll need to use in order to set up the plugin (I've blurred out my own data):

Site information:

Site ID:	
Site key:	
Admin site key:	
DB server:	
Registered:	
API example:	
Private link:	

Copy the **Site ID**, **Site Key**, and **Admin site key**, from the Get Clicky website, and paste them into the Settings of the WordPress plugin.

Clicky Settings

Go to your user homepage on Clicky and click "Preferences" under the name of the domain, you will find the Site ID, Site Key, Admin Site Key and Database Server under Site information.

Site ID:

Site Key:

Admin Site Key:

Advanced Settings

Ignore Admin users: ☑

If you are using a caching plugin, such as W3 Total Cache or WP-Supercache, please ensure that you have it configured to NOT use the cache for logged in users. Otherwise, admin users *will still* be tracked.

Disable cookies: ☐

If you don't want Clicky to use cookies on your site, check this button. By doing so, uniques will instead be determined based on their IP address.

Track names of commenters: ☑

Outbound Link Pattern: _____ For instance:

/out/,/go/

If your site uses redirects for outbound links, instead of links that point directly to their external source (this is popular with affiliate links, for example), then you'll need to use this variable to tell our tracking code additional patterns to look for when automatically tracking outbound links. Read more here.

Make sure the Ignore Admin Users is checked so that your own visits are NOT tracked when you are logged into your Dashboard.

Next click on the **Update Clicky Settings** button at the bottom. That's it, you're all done here.

When someone visits your website, the plugin sends information about that visit to your Get Clicky account.

When you want to check how many visitors you are getting on your site, you can login at Get Clicky and use the tools they provide for visitor analysis. We won't go into more details here about how to use Get Clicky. If you want more help on that, you can read the Help section on their site. Alternatively, you can just go over there and explore the options.

As your site grows, I'd highly recommend you look into Google Analytics and make the switch. It's the best free tool out there and gives a wealth of information about your visitors.

Tasks to complete

1. Set up an account at Get Clicky.
2. Install the Clicky plugin and configure it as above.
3. Go over to the Clicky website and explore the tracking options. Use their Help if needed, so that you can find your way around the data and make sense of what it all means.
4. When you have time, look into Google Analytics.

Search Engine Optimization (SEO)

Search Engine Optimization has changed a lot in the last couple of years. It has always been one of the most important aspects of building a website because it helps you to rank better in Google, and consequently get more traffic and make more sales from your pages (the latter only being important if your site is commercial of course).

Today, things are very different. If you overdo your optimization, Google are likely to penalise you and dump your site out of their search engine.

If you ask Google about the best way to optimize your site, they'd probably tell you to avoid Search Engine Optimization altogether and just focus your efforts on the 'visitor experience', and not to worry about the search engines.

Despite sounding like a lost cause, you should still consider a number of "best practices" as you build your website. I will list the main things to consider here, but if you want a more in-depth discussion about SEO, I'd highly recommend my own book on the subject called **SEO 2014 & Beyond :: Search Engine Optimization will never be the same again.**

It's available in Kindle Format on Amazon:

Search Amazon for: **B0099RKXE8**

Main points for safe SEO

1. Always write content for the visitor, not the search engines.

2. Always create the highest quality content possible and make it unique. More than that, add something to your content that is not found on any other websites covering the same or similar topic, for example, your personal voice, experience or thoughts.

3. Engage your visitor, and allow them to open discussion with you via the built in comments feature.

4. Never try to write content based on keyword phrases. Always write content around a topic. E.g. don't write an article on "best iphone case", write an article on "Which iPhone Case offers the best protection for your phone?" See the difference?

5. As a measure of whether your content is good enough, ask yourself if you could imagine your article appearing in a glossy magazine? If you answer no, then it's not good enough to publish on your own website.

6. DO NOT hire people to build backlinks to your site. If you want to build some links, create them on quality websites that point back to yours. More on this in my SEO book mentioned previously.

7. Add a social sharing plugin to your site so that people can quickly share your content on social channels like Facebook, Twitter, YouTube and Google Plus etc.

The best advice I can give you for present day SEO is to read and digest Google's Webmaster Guidelines. They are there to help us create sites that will rank well in their Search Engine Results Pages, aka SERPs. You can read those guidelines here:

http://goo.gl/PyMip

Wordpress SEO

There are a number of ways you can improve the on-site SEO of your Wordpress site. While some of the basics are included in this book, I wrote a separate comprehensive book on the subject of Wordpress SEO. You can find it by searching Amazon for B00ECF70HU.

Tasks to complete

1. Read Google's Webmaster Guidelines over and over again until you know them off by heart. They really are very important and will benefit you in the long run; providing you adhere to their suggestions of course

235

Where to go from here?

We've covered a lot of ground in this book. You should now be confident finding your way around the WordPress Dashboard.

You have installed WordPress, installed the essential plugins, and configured everything so that your site is now ready for content.

So what's the next step?

Create impressive content!

Everything we have done in this book has been to achieve one main goal. Get your site set up & ready to accept your content. You can now concentrate on publishing content while WordPress takes care of the rest.

Here is your plan going forward.

1. Create a post.
2. Publish it.
3. Rinse and repeat steps 1 and 2.

If you want a "static" homepage rather than one showing your recent posts, create a PAGE with the content you want displayed there. Then set up the reading settings so that this page is shown permanently on your site's front page. You can then go back to the 3-step process outlined above

Create a post, publish & repeat.

I have created a website all about Wordpress where you can find more tutorials or ask me questions. The website is at:

http://rapidwpsites.com

Good luck!

Andy Williams

http://ezSEONews.com

Useful resources

There are a few places that I would recommend you visit for more information.

http://ezSEONews.com – This is my site where I offer free help and advice to webmasters. While you are there, sign up for my free weekly newsletter. You can also look through past issues and read articles on a variety of topics related to building WordPress sites.

SEO 2014 & Beyond :: Search engine optimization will never be the same again (http://goo.gl/rJ6b4)– This is my book on the new SEO. I say the "New SEO" because SEO changed forever in 2012. Many books, websites and courses that are on sale today are way out of date when it comes to SEO. Following their advice could get your site banned in Google. My book is bang up to date.

Google Webmaster Guidelines (http://goo.gl/cRq7a) – this is the webmasters bible of what is acceptable and what is not in the eyes of the world's biggest search engine.

Google Analytics (http://www.google.com/analytics/) – the best free analytics program out there. When you have some free time to learn how to use Google Analytics, I recommend you upgrade from Get Clicky.

Google Webmaster Tools (http://goo.gl/JkGqv) – This is a set of tools built to help webmasters. It is also a route by which Google can send you messages via email if there are any problems or other things you should know about regarding your website.

Please leave a review on Amazon

If you enjoyed this book, or even if you didn't, I'd love to hear your comments about it. You can leave your thoughts on the Amazon website.

If you don't feel you can leave a review, I'd really appreciate it if you could click the Like button, and click some of the tags on the page (or add your own). They are found near the bottom of the page and will help other people find the book when searching Amazon.

The Book on Amazon by searching for **B009ZVO3H6**

My other Kindle books

All of my books are available as Kindle books and paperbacks. You can view them all here:

http://amazon.com/author/drandrewwilliams

Here are a few of my more popular books:

Creating Fat Content

Creating "Fat" Content that can rank and stick in Google

Look inside ↓

Google want to show the best web pages to their users, but what constitutes the "best"?

The answer is quite simple - the best content is the content that the visitors want to see.

Not very helpful? Then read this book. It's packed with advice on what Google actually want, and how you can deliver it with a simple mindset shift - by thinking in terms of "share-bait". That is, content that your visitors want to share with their friends, family and followers. Share-bait will put you on the right path to delivering content that keeps your visitors and search engines happy. It will give you an unfair advantage as your content has a better chance of not only ranking well, but sticking in the search engines.

Creating Web Content is a book packed with ideas, tips and strategies, for creating the most captivating, inspiring and fascinating content for your web site. By keeping your visitors happy, you won't have to worry about search engine algorithm changes, or Google slaps. The search engines will want to show your content to their users.

Search Amazon for **BOOLTZMERM**

Rapid Wordpress Websites

A visual step-by-step guide to building Wordpress websites fast!

Did you ever wish there was a tutorial that would show you just what you needed to know to create your first Wordpress website, without having to wade through stuff you'll never use?

Well this book is that tutorial. It teaches you on a strictly "need-to-know" basis, and will have you building your own website in hours. And I don't leave you stranded either. I created a companion website for readers of this book, with tutorials and help to take your Wordpress skills to the next level, when, and only when, YOU are ready.

What's in this book?

We start at the very beginning by getting good, reliable web hosting and choosing a domain name. I actually walk you through every step, so there will be no confusion.

Once you have your domain, we'll install Wordpress and have a look around the Wordpress Dashboard - think of this as your mission control.

After planning what we want to do, we'll actually build the companion site as we work through the book. We cover the essential settings in Wordpress that you need to know, how to use the editor, the difference between pages and post, categories and tags, etc.

We'll set up custom navigation so your visitors can find their way around your Wordpress site, and carefully use widgets to enhance the design and user experience.

Once the site is built, we'll play around with customizing the look and feel using themes, and I'll point you in the direction of some interesting plugins you might like to look at. These will be covered in more depth on the companion website.

The book will take you from nothing to a complete website in hours, and I'll point out a number of beginner mistakes and things to avoid.

Search Amazon for **B00JGWW86W**

Wordpress SEO

On-Page SEO for your Wordpress Site

Most websites (including blogs) share certain features that can be controlled and used to help (or hinder, especially with Google Panda & Penguin on the loose) with the on-site SEO. These features include things like the page title, headlines, body text, ALT tags and so on. In this respect, most sites can be treated in a similar manner when we consider on-site SEO.

However, different platforms have their own quirks, and WordPress is no exception. Out-of-the-box WordPress doesn't do itself any SEO favours, and can in fact cause you ranking problems, especially with the potentially huge amount of duplicate content it creates. Other problems include static, site-wide sidebars and footers, automatically generated meta tags, page load speeds, SEO issues with Wordpress themes, poorly constructed navigation, badly designed homepages, potential spam from visitors, etc. The list goes on.

This book shows you how to set up an SEO-friendly Wordpress website, highlighting the problems, and working through them with step-by-step instructions on how to fix them.

By the end of this book, your WordPress site should be well optimized, without being 'over-optimized' (which is itself a contributing factor in Google penalties).

Search Amazon for: **B00ECF70HU**

SEO 2014 & Beyond

Search Engine Optimization will Never be the Same Again!

On February 11th, 2011, Google dropped a bombshell on the SEO community when they released the Panda update. Panda was designed to remove low quality content from the search engine results pages. The surprise to many webmasters were some of the big name casualties that got taken out by the update.

On 24th April 2012, Google went in for the kill when they released the Penguin update. Few SEOs that had been in the business for any length of time could believe the carnage that this update caused. If Google's Panda was a 1 on the Richter scale of updates, Penguin was surely a 10. It completely changed the way we needed to think about SEO.

On September 28th 2012, Google released a new algorithm update targeting exact match domains (EMDs). I have updated this book to let you know the consequences of owning EMDs, and added my own advice on choosing domain names. While I have never been a huge fan of exact match domains anyway, many other SEO books and courses teach you to use them. I'll tell you why I think those other courses and books are wrong. The EMD update was sandwiched in between another Panda update (on the 27th September) and another Penguin update (5th October).

Whereas Panda seems to penalize low quality content, Penguin is more concerned about overly aggressive SEO tactics. The stuff that SEOs had been doing for years, not only didn't work anymore, but could now actually cause your site to be penalized and drop out of the rankings. That's right, just about everything you have been taught about Search Engine Optimization in the last 10 years can be thrown out the Window. Google have moved the goal posts.

I have been working in SEO for around 10 years at the time of writing, and have always tried to stay within the guidelines laid down by Google. This has not always been easy because to compete with other sites, it often meant using techniques that Google frowned upon. Now, if you use those techniques, Google is likely to catch up with you and demote your rankings. In this book, I want to share with you the new SEO. **The SEO for 2014 and Beyond.**

Search Amazon for **B0099RKXE8**

An SEO Checklist

A step-by-step plan for fixing SEO problems with your web site

Look inside ⬎
Dr. Andy Williams
kindle edition

A step-by-step plan for fixing SEO problems with your web site

Pre-Panda and pre-Penguin, Google tolerated certain activities. Post-Panda and post-Penguin, they don't. As a result, they are now enforcing their Webmaster Guidelines which is something that SEOs never really believed Google would do! Essentially, Google have become far less tolerant of activities that they see as rank manipulation.

As webmasters, we have been given a choice. Stick to Google's rules, or lose out on free traffic from the world's biggest search engine.

Those that had abused the rules in the past got a massive shock. Their website(s), which may have been at the top of Google for several years, dropped like a stone. Rankings gone, literally overnight!

To have any chance of recovery, you MUST clean up that site. However, for most people, trying to untangle the SEO mess that was built up over several years is not always easy. Where do you start?

That's why this book was written. It provides a step-by-step plan to fix a broken site. This book contains detailed checklists plus an explanation of why those things are so important.

The checklists in this book are based on the SEO that I use on a daily basis. It's the SEO I teach my students, and it's the SEO that I know works. For those that embrace the recent changes, SEO has actually become easier as we no longer have to battle against other sites whose SEO was done 24/7 by an automated tool or an army of cheap labor. Those sites have largely been removed, and that has leveled the playing field.

If you have a site that lost its rankings, this book gives you a step-by-step plan and checklist to fix problems that are common causes of ranking penalties.

Search Amazon for **B00BXFAULK**

Kindle Publishing

Format, Publish & Promote your books on Kindle

Why Publish on Amazon Kindle?

Kindle publishing has captured the imagination of aspiring writers. Now, more than at any other time in our history, an opportunity is knocking. Getting your books published no longer means sending out hundreds of letters to publishers and agents. It no longer means getting hundreds of rejection letters back. Today, you can write and publish your own books on Amazon Kindle without an agent or publisher.

Is it Really Possible to Make a Good Income as an Indie Author?

The fact that you are reading this book description tells me you are interested in publishing your own material on Kindle. You may have been lured here by promises of quick riches. Well, I have good news and bad. The bad news is that publishing and profiting from Kindle takes work and dedication. Don't just expect to throw up sub-par material and make a killing in sales. You need to produce good stuff to be successful at this. The good news is that you can make a very decent living from writing and publishing on Kindle.

My own success with Kindle Publishing

As I explain at the beginning of this book, I published my first Kindle book in August 2012, yet by December 2012, just 5 months later, I was making what many people consider being a full time income. As part of my own learning experience, I setup a Facebook page in July 2012 to share my Kindle publishing journey (there is a link to the Facebook page inside this book). On that Facebook page, I shared the details of what I did, and problems I needed to overcome. I also shared my growing income reports, and most of all, I offered help to those who asked for it. What I found was a huge and growing audience for this type of education, and ultimately, that's why I wrote this book.

What's in this Book?

This book covers what I have learned on my journey and what has worked for me. I have included sections to answer the questions I myself asked, as well as those questions people asked me. This book is a complete reference manual for successfully formatting, publishing & promoting your books on Amazon Kindle. There is even a section for non-US publishers because there is stuff there you specifically need to know. I see enormous potential in Kindle Publishing, and in 2013 I intend to grow this side of my own business. Kindle publishing has been liberating for me and I am sure it will be for you too.

Search Amazon for **B00BEIX34C**

Self-Publishing on Createspace

Convert & Publish your books on Createspace

Self-publishing your own work is easier than at any time in our history. Amazon's Kindle platform and now Createspace allow us to self-publish our work, with zero costs up front.

Createspace is a fantastic opportunity for writers. You publish your book, and if someone buys it, Createspace print it and send it to the customer. All the author needs to do is wait to be paid. How's that for hands-free and risk-free publishing?

This book takes you step-by-step through my own process for publishing. Topics covered include:

- Basic Text Formatting
- Which Font?
- Links and formatting checks
- Page Numbering in Word
- Adding a new title to Createspace
- Price calculator and deciding on Trim size
- Image DPI requirements
- Paint Shop Pro conversion process
- Common formatting problems
- Book Cover Templates
- Creating the cover with Photoshop Elements
- Creating the cover in Paint Shop Pro
- Submitting the book & cover to Createspace
- Expanded Distribution?

The book also includes links to a number of video tutorials created by the author to help you understand the formatting and submission process.

Search Amazon for **B00HG0GE0C**

CSS for Beginners

Learn CSS with detailed instructions, step-by-step screenshots and video tutorials showing CSS in action on real sites

Most websites and blogs you visit use cascading style sheets (CSS) for everything from fonts selection & formatting, to layout & design. Whether you are building WordPress sites or traditional HTML websites, this book aims to take the complete beginner to a level where they are comfortable digging into the CSS code and making changes to their own site. This book will show you how to make formatting & layout changes to your own projects quickly and easily.

The book covers the following topics:

- Why CSS is important
- Classes, Pseudo Classes, Pseudo Elements & IDs
- The Float property
- Units of Length
- Using DIVs
- Tableless Layouts, including how to create 2-column and 3-column layouts
- The Box Model
- Creating Menus with CSS
- Images & background images

The hands on approach of this book will get YOU building your own Style Sheets from scratch. Also included in this book:

- Over 160 screenshots and 20,000 words detailing ever step you need to take.
- Full source code for all examples shown.
- Video Tutorials.

The video tutorials accompanying this book show you:

- How to investigate the HTML & CSS behind any website.
- How to experiment with your own design in real time, and only make the changes permanent on your site when you are ready.

A basic knowledge of HTML is recommended, although all source code from the book can be downloaded and used as you work through the book.

Search Amazon for **B00AFV44NS**

Migrating to Windows 8.1

For computer users without a touch screen, coming from XP, Vista or Windows 7

Review: "What Microsoft should buy and give away now to drive sales"

New PCs are coming pre-installed with Windows 8, Microsoft's new incarnation of the popular operating system. The problem is, the PCs it is installed on are not usually equipped with the piece of hardware that Windows 8 revolves around - a touch screen.

Windows 8 is probably the least user-friendly version of the operating system ever released. It's almost like two different operating systems merged together. From the lack of a start menu, to features that only really make sense on a tablet or phone, Windows 8 has a lot of veteran Windows users scratching their heads. If you are one of them, then this book is for you.

After a quick tour of the new user interface, the book digs deeper into the features of Windows 8, showing you what everything does, and more importantly, how to do the things you used to do on older versions of Windows. The comprehensive "How to" section answers a lot of the questions new users have, and there's also a complete keyboard shortcut list for reference.

If you are migrating to Windows 8 from XP, Vista or Windows 7, then this book may just let you keep your hair as you learn how to get the most out of your computer. Who knows, you may even get to like Windows 8.

Search Amazon for **B00CJ8AD9E**

More information from Dr. Andy Williams

If you would like more information, tips, tutorials or advice, there are two resources you might like to consider.

The first is my free weekly newsletter over at ezSEONews.com offering tips, tutorials and advice to online marketers and webmasters. Just sign up and my newsletter, plus SEO articles, will be delivered to your inbox. I cannot always promise a weekly schedule, but I do try ;)

I also run a course over at CreatingFatContent.com, where I build real websites in front of members in "real-time" using my system of SEO.